MAJOR ADVANCES IN SPACE DISCOVERY
BY UDO BECKER

SIX BIOGRAPHICAL ESSAYS
BY KARL BEDNARIK

THE SPACE FLIGHT PROGRAM
BY WERNHER VON BRAUN

PUBLISHED BY HERDER AND HERDER

DISCOVERERS OF SPACE

A PICTORIAL NARRATION BY ERICH LESSING

PREFACE
BY ARCHIBALD MAC LEISH

INTRODUCTION
BY SIR BERNARD LOVELL

COLOR PHOTOS

Page 9: courtesy of Novosti Press Agency; pages 12–13: copied from originals
in the Austrian National Library; pages 169, 170–171: courtesy of the
National Aeronautics and Space Administration.

BLACK AND WHITE PHOTOS (KEYED BY NUMBERS)

Astronomical Society, London: 79, 80, 81
Austrian National Library, Vienna: 2, 4, 6, 11, 12, 13, 17, 19, 23, 24, 26, 28, 29, 30
32, 35, 37, 39, 43, 46, 47, 52, 55, 56, 57, 61, 69
Berlin City Library, Picture Archives (Handke): 66
Deutsche Presse Agentur: 76
Fürböck, Graz: 33
Wilfried Göpel Archives for Art and History, Berlin: 70, 71
Philippe Halsman, New York: 141
Historia-Photo, Bad Sachsa: 9, 18
Internationale Bilder-Agentur (IBA), Zurich: 85
Keystone, Munich: 77
National Library, Florence: 44
National Library, London: 59, 60, 62, 68
National Library, Paris: 20, 21, 22, 31, 41, 42, 49, 53, 54, 63
Süddeutscher Verlag, Munich: 75, 87
USIS Photo, Bad Godesberg: 78, 86
Photos not listed above are from the Herder Archives.

Albert Einstein's letters on pages 140–141 and 156–157 were taken from
Carl Seelig's book, ALBERT EINSTEIN, by courtesy of Europa Verlag, Zurich.

We thank Otto Nathan, the administrator of Albert Einstein's estate, for
permission to reproduce the letters on pages 154–155 and 158–159.

The frontispiece, pages 2–3: star constellations in the southern and northern sky.
Woodcut by Albrecht Dürer from a star chart (1515) by Johannes Stabius in the
Austrian National Library, Vienna.

Erich Lessing and the publishers wish to express their thanks to all the
parties and agencies who assisted them in collecting photos for this book.

"A Reflection: Riders on Earth Together, Brothers in the Eternal Cold"
by Archibald McLeish appeared originally on page one of the December 25, 1968,
edition of the *New York Times*. Reprinted with the permission of the
New York Times Company and the author.

Introduction © Bernard Lovell 1969.

CONTENTS

UDO BECKER

A PREFACE
BY ARCHIBALD MACLEISH

A Reflection: Riders on Earth Together,
Brothers in the Eternal Cold

Men's conception of themselves and of each other has always depended on their notion of the earth. When the earth was the World—all the world there was—and the stars were lights in Dante's heaven, and the ground beneath men's feet roofed hell, they saw themselves as creatures at the center of the universe, the sole, particular concern of God—and from that high place they ruled and killed and conquered as they pleased.

And when, centuries later, the earth was no longer the World but a small, wet, spinning planet in the solar system of a minor star off at the edge of an inconsiderable galaxy in the immeasurable distances of space—when Dante's heaven had disappeared and there was no hell (at least no hell beneath the feet)—men began to see themselves, not as God-directed actors at the center of a noble drama, but as helpless victims of a senseless farce where all the rest were helpless victims also, and millions could be killed in world-wide wars or in blasted cities or in concentration camps without a thought or reason but the reason—if we call it one—of force.

Now, in the last few months, the notion may have changed again. For the first time in all of time men have *seen* the earth: seen it not as continents or oceans from the little distance of a hundred miles or two or three, but seen it from the depths of space; seen it whole and round and beautiful and small as even Dante—that "first imagination of Christendom"—had never dreamed of seeing it; as the twentieth-century philosophers of absurdity and despair were incapable of guessing that it might be seen. And seeing it so, one question came to the minds of those who looked at it. "Is it inhabited?" they said to each other and laughed—and then they did not laugh. What came to their minds a hundred thousand miles and more into space— "half way to the moon" they put it—what came to their minds was the life on that little, lonely, floating planet: that tiny raft in the enormous, empty night. "Is it inhabited?"

The medieval notion of the earth put man at the center of everything. The nuclear notion of the earth put him nowhere—beyond the range of reason even—lost in absurdity and war. This latest notion may have other consequences. Formed as it was in the minds of heroic voyagers who were also men, it may remake our image of mankind. No longer that preposterous figure at the center, no longer that degraded and degrading victim off at the margins of reality and blind with blood, man may at last become himself. To see the earth as it truly is, small and blue and beautiful in that eternal silence where it floats, is to see ourselves as riders on the earth together, brothers on that bright loveliness in the eternal cold—brothers who know now they are truly brothers.

4

INTRODUCTION

Three hundred and fifty years ago Kepler derived his three laws of planetary motion. He also published a book describing a trip to the moon. The laws governing the motion of the planets around the sun injected order into the age old attempts of man to understand the arrangement and movements of the earth and the planets in the heavens. His description of the lunar trip was a fantasy, today we would describe it as science fiction. Yet in our age the journey has been accomplished by man—an achievement involving scientific knowledge and technological developments entirely beyond the imagination even of the science fiction writers of Kepler's age.

Kepler is remembered in history for his laws of planetary motion. Through a brilliant analytical study of the motions of the planets he arrived at the correct solution without understanding *why* these movements were a natural consequence of the order of nature. Another half-century elapsed before Newton discovered the universal law of gravitation—that between any two bodies in the universe there exists a force of attraction proportional to the product of their masses and inversely proportional to the square of the distance which separates them. Newton's law governs the fall of the apple to the ground and the motion of the earth and planets around the sun. Kepler's three laws of planetary motion appear as a natural consequence of this universal law of gravitation.

In turn Newton also speculated—but not to the extent of Kepler's lunar trip. In a description of the consequences of the gravitational law he asked that we should imagine a cannon ball shot horizontally from a high mountain top. After a while the cannon ball would fall to earth. If the gun were more powerful and the cannon ball was ejected with greater velocity then it would travel further before falling to earth. Imagine a cannon of great power, said Newton, then eventually the ejected cannon ball would not fall to earth but would traverse the entire globe at the height of the mountain top from which it was ejected.

By this equating of the centrifugal and centripetal forces which were a consequence of his law Newton described, in principle, the first artificial satellite of the earth placed in orbit 300 years later when man had achieved a technological power to blast a Sputnik from earth with sufficient velocity to inject it into an orbit 100 miles high where the air resistance was too small to destroy it by friction as would have happened with Newton's hypothetical cannon ball experiment.

Now, today, the timescale has shortened beyond even the possible conception of our own youth. Three hundred years from Newton's law of gravitation to the first artificial earth satellite; but only three and a half years from that small Sputnik to the drama of man's first weightless journey in earth orbit—and, like fiction itself, only another eight years for the mind of common man to become accustomed to the fantasy of the lunar journeys. When Yuri Gagarin first orbited the earth on 12 April 1961 he was acclaimed by millions of ordinary people. During his visit to London a few months after his flight he was entertained by the Royal Society founded in the age of Newton. The President of the Royal Society asked Gagarin if he would accept copies of the works of Newton which the Society had recently published. Gagarin said he would be delighted because "after all if it had not been for Isaac Newton my journey into space would not have been possible". Indeed, Newton's law and the Keplerian laws, which follow as a natural consequence, govern the complex calculations today which man must make in order to fly himself into space. They are the age old basis on which the power of the rockets, the orbits of the spacecraft and the strength of the lunar landing device must be calculated.

But does Newton's law of gravitation apply to the universe as a whole? Newton concluded that this must be the case, and that as a consequence the universe must be infinite in extent. Otherwise, if it were not infinite, then all the stars would fall into the center of that which was finite because of the inverse square law of attraction. The arguments about the finiteness of the universe are as old as man himself. The age of Copernicus, Tycho Brahe, Kepler, Galileo and Newton settled the local problem of the solar system but hardly glimpsed the immensity of the problem of the universe.

When Galileo first looked at the heavens through his small telescope he produced the *observational* evidence in support of the heliocentric conception of Copernicus that the earth was in motion around the sun. The ancient idea of the earth fixed at the centre of the universe had been destroyed, and once the theological and philosophical eruptions had subsided, there was no serious opposition to the view that the earth and planets were in motion around the sun according to the Keplerian laws. But the idea that the sun and the solar system were at the center of the system of stars and therefore of the universe remained firmly fixed in man's mind. After all if we look around us at night when the sky is clear and if we consider the appearance of the stars in the sky with respect to their diurnal and seasonal changes this seems a reasonable belief. Furthermore, do we for one moment see any features in the sky which might suggest that even the visible stars are not the whole of the universe?

In the eighteenth century there were some conjectures—notably by Thomas Wright and Immanuel Kant—that the solar system was not at the centre of the system of stars which we call the Milky Way, but the observational evidence was not yet available. In 1773 Herschel began the construction of his telescopes—he is believed to have made over 500 telescope mirrors of various sizes in ten years—and he eventually produced his historic 48-inch instrument. In 1785 he described his results to the Royal Society and said that as the power of the telescope increases so the observer "perceives that those objects which had been called nebulae are evidently nothing but clusters of stars. He finds their number increase upon him, and when he resolves one nebula into stars he discovers ten new ones which he cannot resolve." In this way the vital observational evidence began to accumulate, but even after Lord Rosse in 1845 had seen and sketched the spiral structure of some of these nebulae with the help of his great 72-inch telescope at Birr Castle in Ireland their true nature was not appreciated. The existence of the solar system at the centre of the Milky Way which was the universe continued to be a working model.

Indeed nearly a quarter of the twentieth century passed before man at last realized that the universe was of greater immensity and complexity than had yet been conceived. The two critical observations were made with the 100-inch telescope on Mt. Wilson in California which came into use in 1918. Harlow Shapley by studying the distribution of the globular clusters produced unambiguous evidence that the stars of the Milky Way were distributed throughout a flattened disc and that the sun is far removed from the centre of the system. The speculations of Wright, Kant and Herschel were at last given an observational and quantitative status. In the intervening years the distance scales have been revised and the contemporary figure of the sizes originally given by Shapley are that the Milky Way is 100,000 light years in diameter with the solar system about 30,000 light years from the central nucleus. The system consists of 100,000 million stars and within this flattened disc they are arranged in a spiral formation.

Within a few years Edwin Hubble produced the critical evidence in support of Herschel's speculation that some of the nebulae were outside this Milky Way system. He observed the Cepheid variable stars in the Andromeda Galaxy M31 and thereby was able to estimate the distance of this object. The revision of the distance scales has again led to a modification of Hubble's figures. Today we regard Andromeda as almost a twin with the Milky Way. That is a galaxy of 100,000 million stars in a flattened spiral structure 100,000 light years in diameter, and at a distance of two million light years from the Milky Way. Immediately it was recognized that many of the nebulosities visible in the large telescopes were extragalactic nebulae and soon it became possible to recognize and photograph galaxies at distances of more than a thousand million light years. Hubble also gave a quantitative meaning to the reddening of the light from these nebulae. He found that this red shift (the shift of the spectral lines to longer wavelengths) was linearly proportional to the distance of the galaxy. Interpreted as a doppler effect this implies that the galaxies are receding from us and from each other at speeds which increase with the distance and which, at the greatest limits of penetration today, amount to significant fractions of the velocity of light. This observed expansion of the universe gave an observational significance to the deductions about the nature of space-time made from Einstein's general theory of relativity.

These developments opened man's eyes to the nature of the cosmological problem. They did not solve the problem, on the contrary the issues are seen to be far more complex than those envisaged by Newton on the basis of his gravitational laws. Now today we live in an age where the radio telescopes and the space probes enable us to view the universe over the entire electromagnetic spectrum. We penetrate to the remote parts of space-time. Our telescopes collect data about the universe as it was many thousands of millions of years ago. We receive radio waves which started out on their journey through space before the earth came into existence, but two great issues still puzzle the intellect of man. How did the universe come into existence, and in what manner did our own solar system evolve? We believe that the great optical and radio telescopes can provide the observational evidence for the settlement of the first problem, and the lunar and space probes for the second. The trouble today is that every time a decisive observation seems to be possible even further difficulties and complexities are revealed. Throughout the ages revealed in this book it seems that in every epoch man has been confident that he understood the universe. Perhaps for the first time in history we do not have this confidence today.

This book is a revelation of the critical stages in the development of man's understanding of the universe. The vivid biographical sketches destroy the familiar myth that the heroic intellects of the past were men favoured by nature and the state. We see them as they were, nearly always in advance of their age, often in intellectual opposition to the contemporary establishment, and surrounded by cynicism and disbelief.

BERNARD LOVELL, O.B.E., F.R.S.,
Professor of Radio Astronomy,
Director of the Experimental
Station, Jodrell Bank.

Right: Man can survive in the open expanses of space. This was proved by the Soviet cosmonaut, Alexei Leonov, on March 18, 1965. For 20 minutes he walke outside Voskhod II, 279 miles out in space.

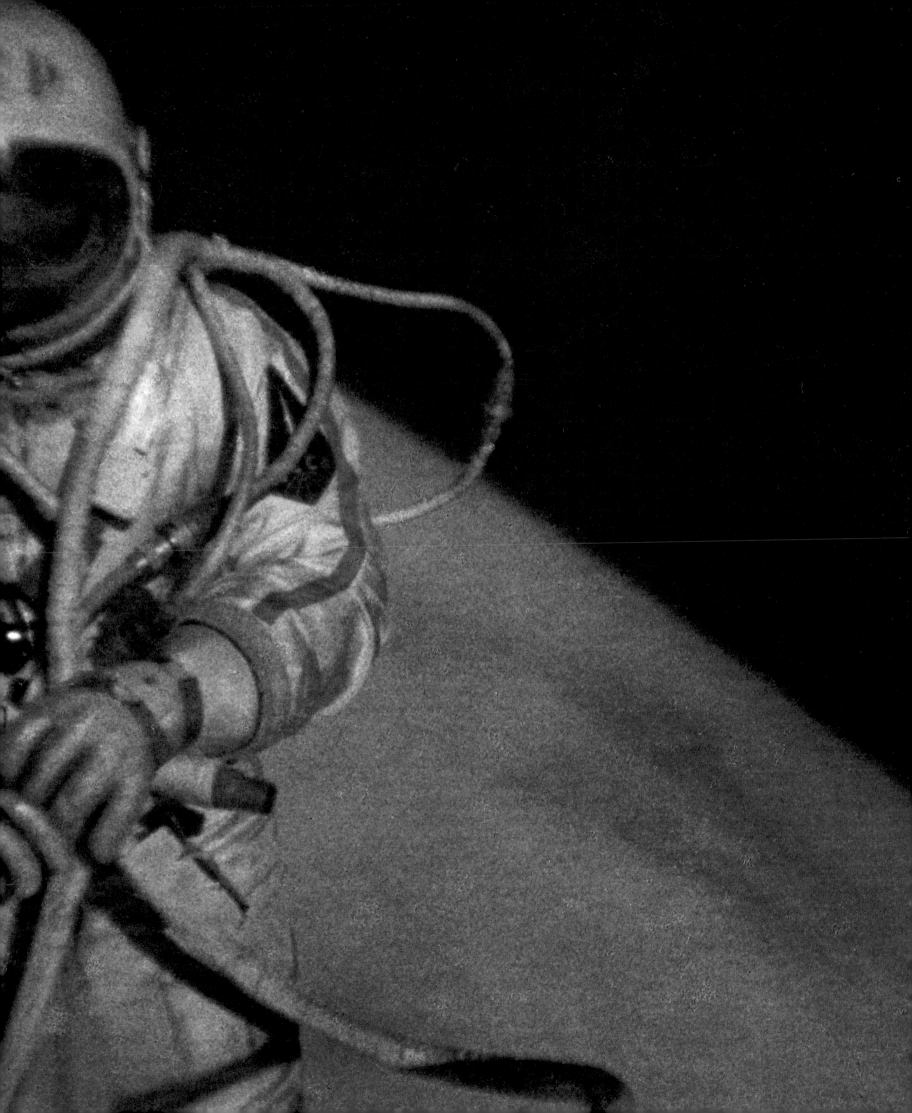

MAN AND THE UNIVERSE

Tethered to his spacecraft by a thin line, Alexei Leonov stepped out of Voskhod II on March 18, 1965, and became the first man to walk in space. His brief jaunt, almost three hundred miles away from earth, was an important milestone in man's conquest of the universe. Though the history of space travel is still young – it began with Yuri Gagarin's trip on April 12, 1961—man's urge to master the secrets of space is of ancient origin.

Ever since man has inhabited this planet, he has gazed in wonder at the star-filled heavens and tried to plumb the laws of the universe. The biblical phrase "He saw the heavens open" represents more than a visionary glimpse of God. It also suggests man's urge to explore his further environment, and reveals his unconfirmed suspicion that the earth and the heavens are bound together by fixed laws.

Man has watched birds soaring towards the sun and fiery meteors plunging to earth at night. Is it any wonder, then, that he has never ceased to entertain the possibility of communication between the earth and the heavens? He has pictured gods and angels coming down to earth, and holy men being carried up to heaven by supernatural powers. He has also dreamed of storming the heavens through his own efforts. Mythology tells us that the first space traveler was Icarus, who went too close to the sun and fell to his doom.

In those early legends, of course, the realm of space was a cozy little place. The earth's atmosphere and the starry skies seemed to be one and the same. The sun, the clouds, and the stars were not too far away from each other. It would need many millennia of close observation before men would arrive at an accurate picture of things.

STAR-GAZING BEGINS

It did not take man long to establish a connection between his life on earth and the course of heavenly phenomena. He soon developed an interest in the celestial bodies which he saw rising and setting at night or during the day. The regular alternation of day and night and the periodic change of seasons profoundly affected nature and man's own life. Every society had need of calendars, in order to know, for example, the right time for sowing and reaping, for procreation and birth, for religious celebrations and obsequies.

Thus calendars appeared very early in human history. The Egyptians developed

1. *Egyptian calendar inscription. From a tomb at Techne, c. 2450* B.C.

2. *The sanctuary at Stonehenge on Salisbury Pla with its standing stones. Some scholars claim tha these stones were positioned according to the cour the sun.*

From a page in the Mayan manuscript at Dresden. The dots and dashes are calendric data.

calendars as early as 4000 B.C.; the Chaldeans and Persians soon followed their example. We know that the Chinese had calendars by 1000 B.C. On the American continent, the Mayas had established a very exact calendar system by 500 B.C.

In most cults and religions, the course of the sun or the phases of the moon or both together played a significant role. Cultic ritual was usually tied up with cosmic processes, so it is not surprising that priests were the first to systematize information gleaned from observation of the heavens. Of course, in the process, the data was adapted to meet cultic requirements. Sound astronomical predictions were intermixed with superstition and myth.

EARLY COSMOLOGIES

The planets were found to be particularly bewildering. While all the other stars seemed to maintain a fixed position, the planets shifted their position at regular intervals. They were roving stars. The most familiar rover was Venus, the morning and evening star; it was the most conspicuous heavenly body after the sun and moon. This planet shines so brightly that it can sometimes be seen on a sunny day. The planet Mercury traverses its heavenly course more quickly than Venus, while Mars, Jupiter, and Saturn move more slowly. All in all, out of approximately 6000 stars visible to the naked eye, five heavenly bodies attracted men's attention because of their relatively quick passage around the heavens.

It took thousands of years, however, for man to devise a fairly accurate picture of these planetary movements and their relationship to the whole celestial system. The main obstacle was that man vastly overrated the position of his own standpoint, earth; a serious distortion in perspective crippled his outlook. Man could not imagine that the earth was only a planet like all the others, and a pretty small one at that.

The ancient Egyptians pictured the universe as a rectangular box, whose bottom was the earth. The early Greeks pictured the earth as a circular disk swimming in water. Later, in Homer's time, they pictured it as a disk suspended in the air. In the sixth century B.C., Pythagoras formulated his conception: the earth was a spherical ball, and the sun, moon, and planets moved around it in accordance with physical laws. The interplay of the planets resulted in the "harmony of the spheres." Two fires, one lodged in the center of the system and one on the outside encircling everything, provided the cosmos with light and air.

It was among the Greeks that the first correct conceptions began to appear somewhat later. The first investigator to put the sun at the center of the planetary system was Herakleides of Pontos (c. 375–310 B.C.), who had studied under Plato and possibly under Aristotle as well. He was convinced that the earth rotated on its axis once a day. He also believed that the two inner planets, Mercury and Venus, revolved around the sun; so he concluded that the earth did the same thing.

Aristarchus of Samos was born the year Herakleides died. After very careful observation, he calculated that the solar year lasted $365\frac{1}{4}$ days; and he worked out

*Hebrew prophets,
kings, and elders
observing the starry heavens.
From a medieval
illuminated manuscript.
Vienna, Austrian
National Library.*

Christian kings
and philosophers of antiquity
observing the heavens.
From a medieval
illuminated manuscript.
Vienna, Austrian
National Library.

a method of calculating the earth's distance from the sun. In one of his works he maintained that the sun is the center of the universe and that all the planets revolve around it. This work is no longer extant; but other Greek thinkers, particularly Archimedes and Plutarch, bear witness to its teachings. The great mathematician Archimedes (287–212 B.C.) tells us that Aristarchus believed that the sun and the fixed stars stood motionless in the heavens while the earth moved in a circle around the sun.

It was only a short step from the conclusions of Aristarchus and Archimedes to the teachings of Copernicus and the formulation of our modern views. But the step was to take a long time, because these conclusions were lost from view in later Greek culture.

PHILOSOPHICAL DETOURS

The influence of philosophy hindered the further development of the natural sciences, for the philosophers claimed priority for their own ideas over the conclusions reached by the natural scientists. Dominant in this respect was the cosmology of the great philosopher Aristotle which once again made the earth the center of the universe. Aristotle considered that God directed the movements of the planets within the "sublunar realm" from some remote vantage point. This realm he placed lower in the order of creation because motion and change took place within it. By contrast the outer realm of apparently fixed stars was divine in nature.

This basic scheme, which was responsible for science's subsequent pursuit of false trails, was given definitive shape by Ptolemy, a Graeco-Egyptian astronomer who lived and worked in Alexandria around A.D. 140. He gave his name to the cosmological outlook that was to hold sway until Copernicus produced his findings many centuries later. In the Ptolemaic system the earth stood fixed and immovable in the center of the universe while this revolved around it, like a complex set of wheels, according to an epicyclic pattern (the epicycle, in which each planet moved, was a circular orbit whose center moved along the circumference of a larger circular path known as the deferent). This epicycle theory dominated the outlook of astronomy for centuries. It was later adopted by the Christian world and was maintained throughout the Middle Ages.

Based exclusively on Scripture, Christianity at first showed no interest in the natural sciences. Cosmology was regarded as a matter of the correct interpretation of Scripture. It had its roots in that of the ancient Babylonians. Thus in Genesis 1, 6 we read: "Then God said, 'Let there be a firmament in the midst of the waters to divide the waters.' And so it was. God made the firmament, dividing the waters that were below the firmament from those that were above it." For a time the earth became a holy tabernacle once again, and the stars were moved around by angels. In the fifth century an anonymous author, since given the name of Pseudo-Dionysius, worked out the whole angelic hierarchy. The most lowly angels have charge of the moon. The archangels handle Venus and Mercury. Angels of the fourth, sixth, and

4. *Ancient cosmological systems and those of Tycho Brahe and Copernicus.*

Fig. I. Ptolemaic System:
The earth in the center, orbited by the moon, Mercury, Venus, the sun, Mars, Jupiter, Saturn, and the realm of fixed stars.

Fig. II. Platonic System:
The earth in the center, orbited by the moon, the sun, Mercury, Venus, Mars, Jupiter, Saturn, and the realm of fixed stars.

Fig. III. Egyptian System:
The earth in the center, orbited by the moon; the sun, orbited in turn by Mercury and Venus, also circles the earth as does Mars, Jupiter, Saturn, and the realm of fixed stars.

Fig. IV. Tychonic System:
The earth in the center, orbited by the moon and sun; the sun in turn is orbited by Mercury, Venus, Mars, Jupiter, and Saturn.

Fig. V. Semi-Tychonic System:
Similar to the Tychonic System; but Jupiter and Saturn orbit the earth, not the sun.

Fig. VI. Copernican System:
The sun in the center, orbited by Mercury, Venus, earth (with its orbiting moon), Mars, Jupiter, and Saturn.

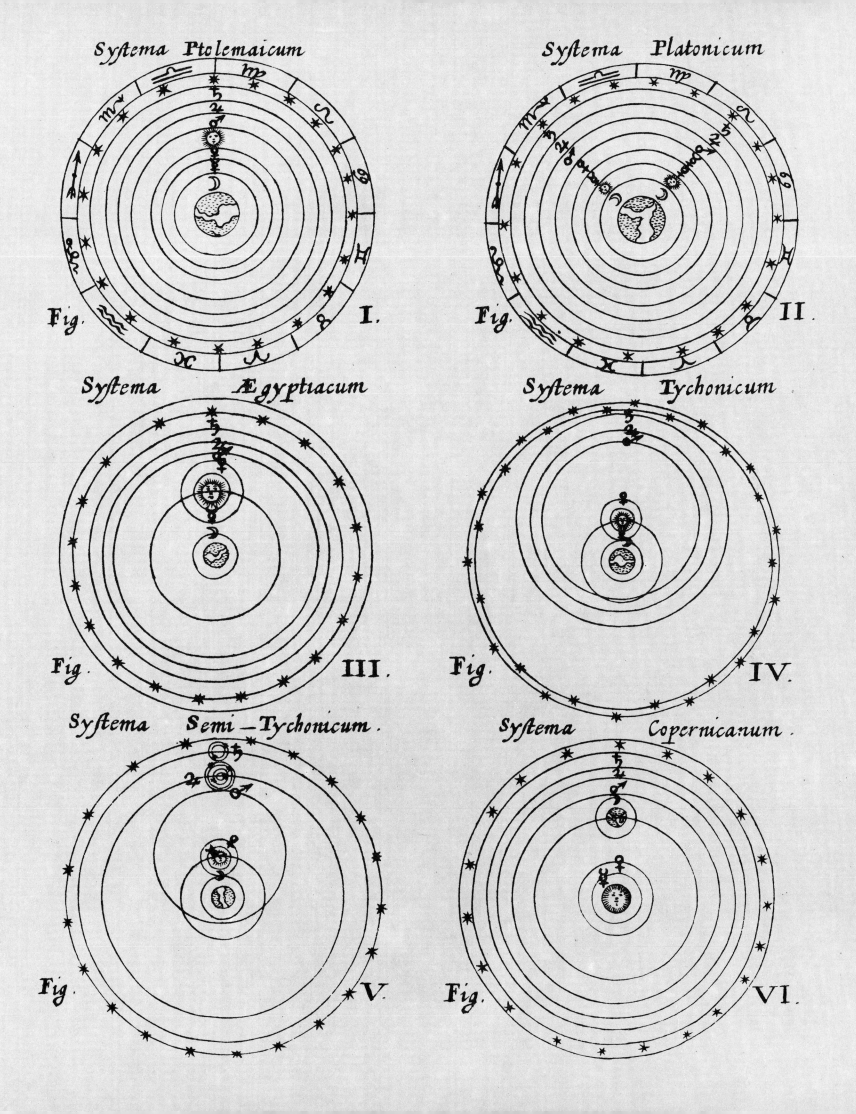

Syſtema Ptolemaicum

Fig. I.

Syſtema Platonicum

Fig. II.

Syſtema Ægyptiacum

Fig. III.

Syſtema Tychonicum

Fig. IV.

Syſtema Semi–Tychonicum.

Fig. V.

Syſtema Copernicanum.

Fig. VI.

seventh rank take care of Jupiter, Mars, and the sun. Angels of the third rank run Saturn, and the Cherubim have charge of the fixed stars. The Seraphim are the triggering motion itself.

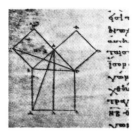
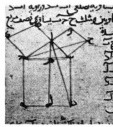
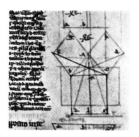

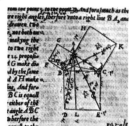

NEW DIRECTIONS

The English Benedictine monk, Bede (674–735), devoted much time to the study of ancient writers and focused attention on theories that had lain forgotten for a long time. It is he who once again propounded the notion that the earth was round. Around the year 1000, this theory won new adherents. From the twelfth century on, the ancient Greek philosophers and scientists were rediscovered. One of the curious twists in this story is that the Greek texts came back to Europe by way of the Arabs; they had to be translated from Arabic into Latin.

So it was that the English monk, Adelard of Bath, discovered an Arabic version of Euclid's *Elements* in Cordova around 1120. Ptolemy's major work, *Almagest,* which had been lost, came back to Europe in Arabic dress — enriched with astrology and superstitious horoscopes. These guidelines for fortune-telling held sway over people for centuries and are still taken seriously today.

Ptolemy's cosmology fitted in nicely with the Christian view of the world. After all, had he not said that the heavenly bodies are not subject to the same laws as earth? In his view they were divine in nature, and there could be no common bond between the earth and the stars. It coincided nicely with Scriptural interpretation.

But this renewed interest in Greek authors also proved beneficial. Scholarship picked up where it had left off centuries before. In the late Middle Ages, a series of outstanding theologians began to think for themselves once again and to propose new ideas to their contemporaries. Two such theologians were the "Doctor universalis," Albertus Magnus (c. 1200–1280), and his famous pupil, Thomas Aquinas (1225–1274). They established a new philosophical foundation for theology. Following the teaching of Aristotle (384–322 B.C.), they held that the universe was a sphere, completely filled with matter and containing no vacuum. The force behind this universe was God, whom Aristotle had called the "unmoved mover," and all motion and effort was directed to him.

Thomas based his proofs for the existence of God on the notion that God, the prime mover, set the heavenly bodies in motion with the help of the angels. This line of argument was promptly attacked by some of his contemporaries. At Oxford, William of Ockham (c. 1300–1349) pointed out that some physical impulses operated at a distance without any direct contact — e.g. magnetism.

Nonetheless, Aristotelianism did contribute a measure of empirical observation and critical examination to the prevailing Platonic outlook, which had been highly abstract and speculative. A sudden enthusiasm for concrete experimentation broke to the surface. The Franciscan, Roger Bacon (c. 1220–1292), who taught at Oxford, set down this ideal: "The true scientist must subject all things in heaven and under

5. The theorems of Pythagoras were known throughout the civilized world in the sixteenth century. Above: editions in various languages.

6. Arabic astronomer. From an illuminated manuscript of the Almagest.

16

*Roger Bacon, Doctor mirabilis, was the leading
thinker in the natural science school at Oxford. He
regarded experimentation as the only guarantee of truth.*

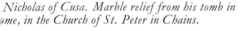

*Nicholas of Cusa. Marble relief from his tomb in
Rome, in the Church of St. Peter in Chains.*

it to experiment. He should blush to find out that he does not know something about the earth that the average person does know."

From his own experiments Bacon became convinced that man could construct self-propelling vehicles, submarines, and airships. He also criticized those who blindly followed older authorities: "If I had my way, I would burn all the writings of Aristotle. For the study of Aristotle is a waste of time; it propagates error and ignorance." Aristotle himself would probably have agreed with these sentiments, if he could have seen the blind reverence in which his opinions were held. Bacon, at any rate, was censured by his Order and put under close surveillance.

Thus scholastic philosophy, based upon the teaching of Aristotle, remained the dominant philosophy. Natural observation all too quickly became theological speculation. Instead of heeding Aristotle's advice to study nature directly, scholars quoted Aristotle as the final authority on all questions dealing with nature.

SEEDS OF A NEW COSMOLOGY

The new current of thought was not to be stopped. New viewpoints arose, paving the way for the revolutionary events which we call the "Renaissance" and the "Reformation." Both events resulted from the impact of humanism, which may be regarded as the great intellectual revolution in modern history.

The Italian poet and humanist, Angelo Poliziano (1454–1494), did much to foment the humanist spirit. He was one of the first humanists to study the ancient texts with a critical eye. He started a modern philosophy, based directly on the classical texts themselves rather than on the commentaries of theologians. North of the Alps, Johann Reuchlin (1455–1522) carried on this work after Poliziano's death.

The German Cardinal, Nicholas of Cusa (1401–1464), combined theological and scientific speculation in a startlingly original way. His approach and his ideas provided the strongest impetus for the development of a new cosmology. He asserted that the earth could not be the center of the universe, because the center of the universe would have to be the Absolute — namely, God; nor were the heavens more perfect than the earth. He thought it was possible that the heavenly bodies were inhabited by living beings similar to those on earth. Basing his views on those of the English philosophers, he was of the opinion that at creation God gave an "impetus" to every heavenly body, and that this initial impetus kept them in motion. He imputed ignorance to all those who believed that the earth stood still: "If a man were to stand on any heavenly body — the earth, the sun, or some other star — his standpoint would always seem to be the motionless center and everything else would seem to be in motion around it." Nicholas of Cusa was also the first philosopher since the Greeks to give mathematics a primary place in philosophical methodology. He was the first to make a dent in the frozen medieval universe.

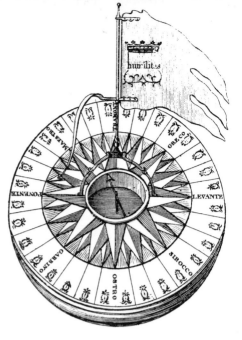

New technological advances contributed a great deal to the development of new ideas. Several inventions had a marked impact on the times.

Gunpowder appeared in Europe in the thirteenth century. We find the first written mention of it in the works of Roger Bacon. It began to have practical use when men started to cast bronze and iron canons.

The magnetic compass also appeared in Europe in the thirteenth century, as a means of indicating directions at sea. Soon after, the Jacob's staff was introduced to help sailors take reckonings at sea.

In the fifteenth century the printing press was invented. By the end of the century there were over a thousand such presses in Europe, and twelve million books had been printed.

9. Compass of Martin Behaim (1436–1507).

The introduction of Jacob's staff and the compass, combined with improvement

10. Printing press in Gutenberg's day. Woodcut.

*. Arrival of the Spaniards in America. Woodcut from the title
ge of a pamphlet printed in Florence in 1493.*

ship construction, enabled sailors to venture away from the coast and undertake
ong voyages in the open sea, for they had learned how to determine their position
y the stars.

Many adventurous souls were ready to take advantage of this new situation, hoping
conquer the world. Columbus was not the only adventurer around. The Portuguese
ad already rounded the southern tip of Africa. Scarcely five years after Columbus's
rst landing in America, Vasco da Gama successfully sailed the sea route to India.
orth America, Brazil, and the Pacific Ocean were discovered soon afterwards.
nly a quarter of a century later, in 1522, Magellan's ship returned from the first
rcumnavigation of the globe. In the same year Cortez conquered Mexico, and
izarro was soon to conquer the Incas of Peru.

In Europe itself, the Reformation had begun. Luther (1483–1546) had formulated
is theses and defended them before the Diet. Local communities were starting to
efect from the papacy. Two forerunners of this movement were the English reformer
ohn Wyclif (1320–1384) and the Czech reformer Jan Hus (who had been burned at
e stake in 1415).

The intellectual roots of the Reformation, too, lay in humanism. During this

*12. Erasmus of Rotterdam.
From an engraving (1526) by
Albrecht Dürer.*

period outstanding figures spent their time in critical examination of newly discovered Greek texts. Thanks to the efforts of these humanists, ancient texts were read once more and examined critically; up to then they had been the exclusive province of theologians. The guiding light of this new era was Erasmus of Rotterdam (1467–1536). His major preoccupation was the study of the original Greek text of the New Testament. In 1516 he published his celebrated new edition of the New Testament in Greek, with an accompanying version in Latin.

Erasmus exerted an enormous influence on his contemporaries. His books were bestsellers for centuries. The file of letters written by or to him numbers in the thousands. During the course of his life, he made contact with all the great centers of Europe: Basle, Bologna, Cambridge, Freiburg, London, Louvain, Oxford, Paris, Rome, and Venice. He had countless friends among the important men of his day. Without exaggeration he could number among his pupils "the emperor, the kings of England, France, and Denmark, Prince Ferdinand of Germany, the Cardinal of England, the Archbishop of Canterbury, and countless princes, bishops, scholars, and reputable men in England, Flanders, France, Germany, Poland, and Hungary."

As has happened with many reformers, Erasmus's activities did not produce the result he had intended. The Reformation squashed the dream of reconciliation which he had cherished. Instead of a Christian humanism, there arose the Counter-Reformation. Humanism continued to make headway within the Reformation, but Catholicism was excluded from the process.

During this same period political events were taking place that were to mark the

13. A Protestant preacher and a Catholic preacher addressing their congregations. Woodcut by G. Pencz for Hans Sachs's poem on the "Two Schools of Preaching" (1529).

20

In the illustration (woodcut), the following labels appear:

Ⱥ Engel · Ⱥ Propheten · Das grab der hey/ligen schrifft. · 匡 Aposteln · hutten. · Reuelatus ē homo, pcti, filius pditiõis, & abominatio, quē percuffit deus virga oris fui. · ℌ Euangeliften · Carloftat · Luther.

Regi autē fcforū imortali inuifibili, foli deo honor & głia in fcła feculorū Amē.

Ego fum via veritas & vita, Iohan. 10.

TRIVPHVS VERITATIS.

4. The victorious Luther returns triumphantly with the sacred Scriptures, which he has recaptured from the "Turks of Rome." The Apostles and Patriarchs carry the Scriptures in a shrine. Ulrich von Hutten drags behind him the Antichrist's captive flock. At the end of the procession is Christ's triumphant cortege. Woodcut from the Reformation period.

5. Drummer and ensign in the peasant army during the Peasants' War. Engraving (1544) by Hans Sebald Beham.

end of the Holy Roman Empire. The common Western heritage of *Imperium* and *Sacerdotium,* Emperor and Papacy, would be left behind. The last knight, Emperor Maximilian (1459–1519), still held the throne; but he was the first emperor to be chosen by the princes instead of by the Pope. His kingdom was weak, disunited, and filled with unrest. Islamism, the politically oriented religion created by Mohammed (c. 570–632), seemed unstoppable. Islamic forces had taken Byzantium and marched into the center of Europe. They were heading towards Vienna and reached the imperial town in 1529.

In this epoch the bankers and merchants asserted their economic independence. In Florence the family of bankers known as the Medici were at the height of their power. The trading city of Venice was powerful enough to declare war on Maximilian. In Augsburg, the merchant family of Fugger was rich enough to finance the Emperor's war against Venice and to buy the subsequent election of Emperor Charles V. Farther north, in Lübeck, Hamburg, and Bruges, the Hanseatic League was at the height of its economic power. In 1531 the first Stock Exchange was set up, in Antwerp. The middle class, represented by the traders and merchants, assumed a major role in history.

The lower middle class, represented by the craftsman and the peasant farmer, did not fare so well when it took its first steps into the political arena. Once again, it was the current of contemporary ideas that led them to seek freedom from the tutelage of the Church and the nobility. Scholars and artists had begun to use the vernacular language and to interpret the biblical events in a way the people could understand. The young Holbein designed his woodcuts for "The Dance of Death," and Lucas

21

Cranach depicted the life of the people on his altar-pieces. Humanist scholars like Reuchlin wrote in the vernacular.

Then the revolt of the little man began. Peasant unrest, flickering beneath the surface since the turn of the century, flared up into open warfare. Luther welcomed this turn of events at first, but later condemned the peasants who were seeking their share of the newly won freedom. Abandoned by the spiritual leaders of the Reformation, thousands of peasants perished in a lost cause; but the Reformation succeeded nevertheless. Local princes then pressed for political independence from the Pope and the Emperor.

All these developments rose out of the new spirit which pervaded the times. Sometimes they paralleled or reinforced each other; sometimes they ran counter to each other. But if we really want to understand this new spirit, we cannot overlook the artistic revolution that helped to shape the Renaissance.

The spirit of antiquity came to life once again. After more than a thousand years of neglect, ancient classical themes were picked up once again and the naked human body was depicted on canvas. Heinrich Heine's point is well taken: "The Italian painters waged a more effective campaign against clericalism than did the theologians of Saxony. The glowing bodies in Titian's works are witnesses to Protestantism. The curves of his Venus are more basic theses than those which Luther nailed to the cathedral door."

The great Italian painters were also revolutionaries, fighting for artistic freedom and creative individualism. They freed themselves from society and sought to create something new. They liberated art from the tutelage of the Church.

Leonardo's "Mona Lisa" has her gaze fixed on new and distant horizons. Da Vinci was also one of the first engineers, and he tried to solve the problems involved in aerodynamics, underwater vessels, and telescopes. Along with the great doctors of his time, he sought to advance man's exploration of the human body. His later artistic works are fragmentary glimpses of some great cosmic vision: cosmic catastrophes, floods, falling meteors, and stellar explosions.

To sum up, the age of Copernicus was full of new and explosive forces: humanism, the Renaissance, the Reformation, social emancipation, great explorations. The time was ripe for a new look at the universe.

16. Man catches a glimpse of new horizons. Sixteenth-century woodcut depicting the new vision of Nicholas of Cusa.

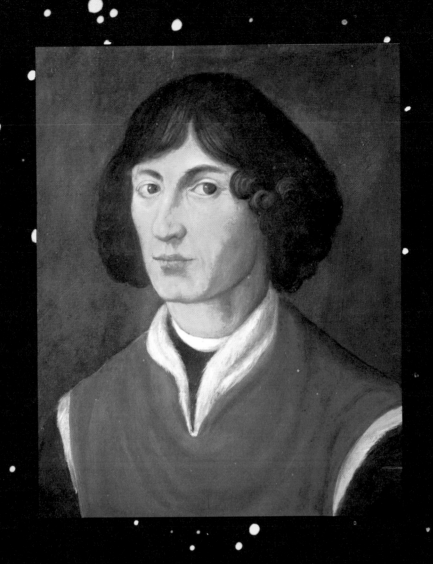

NICHOLAS COPERNICUS

Born: February 1473 in Thorn   Died: May 1543 in Frauenburg

"HE HAS EXPLORED THE SWIFT COURSE OF THE MOON, THE
CHANGING MOTIONS OF THE BROTHERLY STARS, AND THE
WHOLE FIRMAMENT WITH THE PLANETS — THE WONDROUS
CREATION OF OUR FATHER IN HEAVEN. BASING HIS STUDY
ON ASTONISHING PRINCIPLES, HE IS ABLE TO SEEK OUT
THE HIDDEN CAUSES OF THINGS."

Foreword of Laurentius Corvinus to Copernicus's translation of *Theophylactos*

*The preceding page shows a portrait of
Copernicus from the old University of Cracow.*

*Right: At the University of Cracow Copernicus
encounters astronomical instruments for the first
time: a star globe (right), an astrolabe (top),
and a quadrant (left). He really put them to
use for the first time in Italy, the home of humanism,
which exerted an irresistible attraction on him.*

Copernicus studied geometry in this classroom at the University of Cracow. On the walls are geometric figures derived from Euclid's "Elements." From his seat by the window the teacher pointed to the geometric figures with his stick. Like his fellow pupils, Copernicus brought his own stool, writing bench, wax tablet, and block of wood to heat the classroom.

Next page: Four years later Copernicus discovered his true calling. On the roof of the observatory at the University of Bologna, he used his quadrant to observe an eclipse of the moon. Alongside the quadrant lie the Alfonsine planetary tables; Alfonso X of Castile had them assembled (1248–1252) by Arabic, Jewish, and Christian scholars. Beside the planetary tables is an early edition of the "Almagest."

29

Left: After living in Bologna Copernicus moved to the University of Padua to study medicine. In this Anatomy Hall, the first dissections took place; but many superstitious remedies were still prescribed for the ailing patient.

Below: After fourteen years of study, Copernicus returned to Poland. As the canon and physician of his uncle, the Bishop of Ermland, he worked in Heilsberg. The castle was the bishop's residence and a fortress. The bishop was a warrior, as much at home with sword and banner as with chasuble and gospel book.

For thirty years Copernicus lived and worked in Frauenburg. His workroom was in this corner turret of the castle. On clear nights he made his occasional observations with his modest instruments, standing in the courtyard or on the balcony.

Next page: In his book "De revolutionibus orbium coelestium" Copernicus placed the sun at the center of our planetary system. The hole his compass left in the page is clearly visible. This manuscript inaugurated a new epoch, but its author did not dare to propound his views.

THE RELUCTANT REVOLUTIONARY

It was May 24, 1543. Canon Nicholas Copernicus was lying on his death bed in Frauenburg, East Prussia. He had been confined to bed for six months by an attack of apoplexy. For weeks he had not been in his right mind. In a lucid moment shortly before his death, he saw for the first time a printed copy of his new and major work *De revolutionibus orbium coelestium (On the Revolutions of the Heavenly Spheres)*. This work revolutionized man's picture of the universe and ushered in the "Copernican revolution." It put an indelible mark on the outlook of the modern era.

Why did this work come out in print so shortly before the scholar's death? It had been around for some time; apart from some minor corrections, it was already complete seventeen years earlier. Its basic ideas had been worked out and formulated around 1512. The ideas appear in a shorter earlier work known to scholars as the *Commentariolus;* hand-written copies of this earlier work had been circulating among them for many years. In *Commentariolus* he had challenged the Ptolemaic system and set forth seven basic axioms for a more adequate cosmology:

1. The heavenly bodies do not all move around the same center.
2. The earth is not the center of the universe. It is only the center of the moon's orbit and of gravity.
3. The center of the planetary system (hence of the universe) is the sun.
4. The distance of the earth from the sun is infinitesimally small when compared with its distance from the fixed stars.
5. The daily alternation of day and night is due to the earth's rotation on its own axis.
6. The yearly shifts of the sun are due to the fact that the earth rotates around the sun.
7. The apparent shifts and alternations of the planets are also due to their rotation around the sun.

Copernicus also asserted that he would present mathematical proofs for his axioms and his whole system. This promise aroused great interest among his contemporaries. Popes asked to have the theory explained to them, Luther knew the broad outlines of it, and students passed copies from hand to hand. Year after year, however, Copernicus stayed quietly in the background. Only shortly before his death did he permit his major work to be printed.

Copernicus was probably the most reluctant revolutionary of all time. His major work became the centerpiece of the modern intellectual revolution, quite against the will of its author. The revolution of Copernicus was not his revolution at all; it was carried through by the revolutionary spirit of the age. He did all he could to hide the ideas that were to determine the new outlook.

This is all the more surprising when we consider what his contemporaries were doing. Copernicus lived in an age of rebels, explorers, and innovators. He was twenty when Columbus discovered America, twenty-five when Vasco da Gama sailed around Africa to reach India, and forty-nine when Magellan's last ship arrived home from its trip around the world. Now there was concrete, practical proof that the earth was round.

These events did not go unnoticed in Europe. People took a lively interest in them, and news spread quickly. Book printing had become a booming business. From the age of thirty-five on, Copernicus lived in the castle at Frauenburg—on the margin of the civilized world. But he was well aware of the earth-shaking events that were taking place elsewhere.

Copernicus was born on February 19, 1473 in Thorn, a town on the Vistula, in what is now Poland. This ancient outpost of the Teutonic Knights had already become a flourishing trade center and an important member of the Hanseatic League. Its tradesmen, scholars, and clerics traveled widely, and the young Copernicus caught echoes of the new spirit that was abroad. Copernicus himself traveled quite a bit after getting his elementary schooling at Thorn and Chelmo. He was able to pick up the knowledge which his age had to offer, and to broaden his perspectives by travel.

Thus Copernicus was able to form an opinion about the revolutionary events taking place. When Martin Luther nailed his theses to the door of the castle church, Wittenberg, in 1517, Copernicus was able to follow the course of this youthful revolt against the Pope. While he, like his contemporaries, may have failed to perceive the underlying relationship between humanism, the Renaissance, and the Reformation, he could follow the course of external events: the fall of the Holy Roman Empire, the emancipation of the nobility, the merchant revolution, and the peasant uprisings. He could see that all these events were somehow related, even though his own reaction was to adopt an attitude of cautious prudence.

17. Three times in 1517 the Elector of Saxony, Frederick the Wise, dreamt about Martin Luther nailing his theses to the door of the Wittenberg church. Woodcut (1617).

THE STUDENT

His own process of development must be carefully noted. The fact that he early became a ward of his maternal uncle, Bishop Lucas Watzelrode of Ermland, was to be important for his later development. His uncle, who took the youngster in when his parents died, made provisions for his education and financed his travels. At the age of twenty-four, Copernicus took over a vacated canonry in Frauenburg. Without having to receive higher Orders or to remain in a fixed domicile, he was able to enjoy the wealth of a comfortable benefice for many years.

When Columbus landed in America, Copernicus was already a student at the renowned University of Cracow. One of his important teachers at that university

8. *Conrad Celtes presents his works to Emperor Frederick III. Woodcut (1501).*

9. *The Astrologer. Engraving (1509) by Giulio Campagnola.*

was Brudzewski, an astronomer and mathematician. He taught Copernicus "the certainty of mathematical knowledge, keen observation, and the noble simplicity of carefully worked out proofs."

In Copernicus's day, Brudzewski lectured on Aristotle at the university. Scholars say that Copernicus studied mathematics and astronomy under him, because most of the mathematics and astronomy teachers at Cracow then had been his pupils. Sixteen professors lectured on Euclid, arithmetic, optics, the theory of ellipses, Peuerbach's planetary theories and Regiomontanus's astronomy tables. Interestingly enough, only two of them taught astrology.

Conrad Celtes played a special role at Cracow University. He had come there to study under Brudzewski, but he soon began to lecture on poetry and rhetoric. He was already renowned in his own right; his Latin verses, in the manner of Ovid, were some of the best in his day. He had been made the first German poet laureate. Celtes stayed at Cracow for only two years, but his influence on the university lasted for many years. When Copernicus arrived at the university, Celtes had already moved on to Ingolstadt; but Copernicus came under the influence he had exerted on Cracow.

Later, Copernicus went on to study at the universities of Bologna and Padua. It is almost certain that there Copernicus became familiar with the novel ideas of Cardinal Nicholas of Cusa. The influence of the latter followed Copernicus through several universities, but it was probably strongest at the University of Bologna, where Copernicus studied under Novara, the astronomer, and made his first precise observations of the stars. Here traditional astronomy and new ideas must have come to a head for the young student. Novara had been a pupil of Johannes Müller (1436–1476), otherwise known as Regiomontanus, who was summoned to Rome by Pope Sixtus IV to assist in reforming the calendar. Regiomontanus, in turn, had been a pupil of the Austrian astronomer, Georg von Peuerbach (1423–1461), whose planetary theories were known to Cardinal Cusa, his teacher.

Not all of these astronomers espoused the notion of a heliocentric universe, but they were well versed in the theories of the ancient, pre-Ptolemaic Greek astronomers. Regiomontanus studied Aristarchus; and Peuerbach, despite his own conservative views, spearheaded debates on "the earth's motion" in Vienna. Both Copernicus and Galileo studied extracts from the *Almagest* as edited by Peuerbach.

We do not know whether Copernicus earned a degree in astronomy. All we have is his doctoral diploma in Canon Law, which he earned in Ferrara after fourteen years of study. During this period, when he was twenty-seven, Copernicus gave a course of lectures on mathematics in Rome. There he saw the notorious Alexander VI ascend the papal throne in 1500. There can be no doubt that Copernicus drank in the spirit of his age.

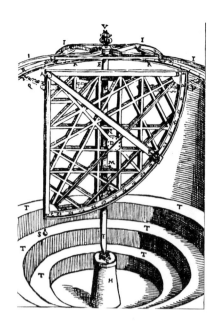

For a long time Copernicus was more esteemed as a doctor than as an astronomer. He served as his uncle's personal physician for many years, even though it is very doubtful that he ever earned a doctoral degree in medicine. All the important early portraits of him, however, depict him with the lily-of-the-valley which was the doctor's symbol. It is also certain that he rendered medical services to other bishops and prelates.

Copernicus was not a great physician. He made no important contribution to the theory or practice of medicine. As in the field of astronomy, contemporary medicine was a hopeless potpourri of medieval notions and natural science. Superstition played a large role in it. The doctor felt his patient's pulse, examined his urine, and then prescribed rather questionable medications. Surgery, like purging, bloodletting, and tooth-pulling, was left to barbers. The use of tried and true household medicines probably accounted for the occasional success of these procedures.

In Padua, where Copernicus studied medicine, new approaches were being introduced in the study of anatomy. Leonardo da Vinci worked up his anatomical studies for the courses at Padua, but Copernicus was out of touch with these innovations. His study of medicine was quite conventional, and one of his prescriptions contains the typical ingredients of the day: ivory scrapings, red sandalwood, unicorn's horn, etc.

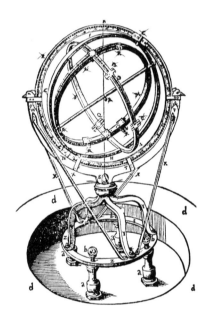

Only on one point does Copernicus the doctor evince a modern spirit: he does not seem to relate medical notions with astrology. This in itself is quite surprising, because most doctors in his day related bodily sickness to cosmic happenings.

THE HUMANIST

At first glance it may seem surprising that Copernicus first spelled out his theories in a book that had nothing to do with astronomy. The book indicated two important things: (1) Copernicus's intellectual roots lay deep in humanism; (2) we can only understand his varied activities (as lawyer, astronomer, doctor, etc.), when we recall that Copernicus was first and foremost a humanist.

Copernicus wrote the book three years after he had returned from Italy. At the time, his career as his uncle's physician was at its height. At first reading, it seems to be a detour into the realm of belles-lettres, for it was the first Latin translation of a Greek work to appear in Eastern Europe. It was another eleven years before lectures on Greek literature and grammar were instituted at Cracow University.

The text itself, a work by the Byzantine historian Theophylactos, was not of major importance. Today we could hardly share Copernicus's enthusiasm for it. If we do not bear in mind the wide ramifications of the humanist movement, we might well wonder why Copernicus got involved with it. The important point is that in this humanistic work we find the first reference to Copernicus's novel theories. The introductory remarks of Laurentius Corvinus, cited on a previous page, bear clear testimony to them.

These remarks indicate that Copernicus was already at work on his system and that he had discussed his ideas with his friends. Three years later his *Commentariolus* appeared, describing his theories for the first time.

THE CANON

But Copernicus was not yet the famous astronomer. After the death of his patron in 1512, Copernicus took on his duties as one of Frauenburg's sixteen canons (he had held the title since 1497). A canon was a provincial nobleman, who had a horse and two servants at his disposal; he also bore arms. His chief duties were administrative, and he wielded almost unlimited authority over the estates of the cathedral chapter. Only one of the canons received Major Orders and was able to say Mass. Today we would call them "managers". Thus Copernicus did not simply lead the quiet life of a scholar. He served as an accountant, developed a monetary theory for Poland, built forts and canals, and served in a judicial capacity.

As Protestantism spread through Prussia and Poland, Copernicus stayed on the sidelines and did not champion either side in the dispute. He was not against the Catholic Church, nor was he against the Reformation. Instead, he tried to mediate between the opposing factions. Through his friend Tiedemann Giese, who was to become Bishop of Ermland, Copernicus had close ties with the ideas of Erasmus. Giese venerated the works of Erasmus, and he heartily endorsed his call for internal Church reform and for a reconciliation between Church dogma and the new advances in knowledge. There can be no doubt that Copernicus was in close contact with these ideas.

While the king of Poland, loyal to Rome, quarelled with the Teutonic Order, which had sided with Protestantism, most of the canons retreated to the fortress of Allenstein. Copernicus became one of the castle's defenders against the Teutonic Order. For a whole year, Ermland was disputed by the Protestant Prussians and the Catholic Poles. The then Bishop of Ermland, who had succeeded Copernicus's uncle, vacillated in his loyalties.

THE ASTRONOMER

By 1514 Copernicus's reputation as an astronomer was already sufficient to earn him an invitation to Rome where the Pope and his advisers needed his assistance in the reform of the calendar. We do not know what Copernicus's exact reply was, but he refused the invitation. Already he had become the hesitant scholar. Later he claimed that his researches were not sufficiently developed to justify calendary reform. Before this could be done, the exact course of the sun and moon would have to be measured. But Copernicus tarried over this exacting task for many years.

As an astronomer, Canon Copernicus remained a conservative in his methods. Despite his good income, he spent little on astronomical instruments. Useful instruments were available to him—astrolabes, quadrants and armillary spheres—but he contented himself with crude, self-made devices. One was the twelve-foot high triquetrum which consisted of three pine-wood poles of which one, provided with sights, hinged on the first, and was used for moon and star sightings. The third was an adjustable and graduated cross-piece from which angles could be read. Copernicus also used a simple quadrant to measure the sun's height at noon, and the well-known Jacob's staff that was used by navigators. It is not surprising that he could only make rough measurements with such instruments.

Copernicus would have been lucky to keep his margin of error under 10 minutes of arc, but he did not succeed in doing this. Moreover, he himself made very few observations of the stars—about seventy in all. In his major work, he refers to only twenty-seven observations of his own; his calculations are based mainly on the observations of earlier astronomers.

The publication of his magnum opus in his own lifetime was due to the enthusiasm of a young mathematician, Georg Joachim von Lauchen. In the humanist tradition it was customary to give scholars Latin nicknames, and the young mathematician was nicknamed Rheticus. At twenty-two Rheticus obtained a chair of mathematics and astronomy in Wittenberg. In 1539 he went to see Copernicus at Frauenburg. Together with Giese, who was now Bishop of Ermland, he persuaded Copernicus to let him see the magnum opus which Copernicus had finished ten years earlier. Rheticus then set about writing his own report, the *Narratio prima,* in which he discussed the theories of "the learned Doctor Nicholas of Thorn." (Copernicus would not permit him to use his real name.)

The report was finished within a year of Rheticus's arrival. Several months later it was published in Danzig, the nearest city with a printing press. Rheticus immediately sent copies to all the big names who would be interested in such a work, including Melanchthon and the Duke of Prussia. Gassarus, a scholar in Basle, brought out a second edition some weeks later.

Rheticus returned to Wittenberg briefly to give a series of lectures, and then hastened back to Frauenburg. He spent more than a year making a copy of Copernicus's major work. He brought this copy to Germany, where it was finally printed in 1542.

Copernicus did not display much thanks for this yeoman's service. Presumably angered by the fuss about getting the book into print, he did not even mention Rheticus's name in the introduction. That is probably why Rheticus did not become his intellectual heir and why he let his biography of Copernicus disappear. Copernicus's life, it seems, ended on a sour note.

23. Anatomy hall. Frontispiece to a book containing a compendium of Andreas Vesalius's writings.

The motives behind Copernicus's reticence towards his own discoveries are shrouded in mystery. Was the great scholar too timid to champion the truth? Or was he prudent enough to see that his work might be used as a weapon in the schism then wracking the Church? Or was he afraid he might be held responsible for subverting the traditional views of Christianity?

One could certainly argue for this view. The Church was preparing to deal a death-blow to the Protestant reformers. Although many learned humanists were still active within the Church, the forces of conservatism were a power to be reckoned with. The Inquisition had been in existence for several centuries, and it had dealt mercilessly with the Albigensians and the Cathari.

On the other hand, the Copernican theory was in no way tied up with the Protestant schism. Luther ridiculed the "nonsensical" views of the "imbecile" in Frauenburg, and Melanchthon urged that he be investigated by the police. The reformers, who demanded freedom of conscience from the Pope, were no less dogmatic in their theology.

When scientific research and artistic freedom seemed to affect the basic tenets of the faith, they were viewed with great suspicion. Copernicus himself never suffered persecution, but he was wise enough to see what might happen if he propagated his theories.

To portray Copernicus as a lone wolf, however, would be quite inaccurate. Loyal friends stood by him throughout his life. Important and highly placed clerics expressed sincere interest in his system. In 1533, Pope Leo X asked for a detailed report on it, and he was favorably impressed. In 1536 Cardinal Schönberg, the Pope's trusted friend, urged Copernicus to make his work public:

> I hear that you not only are thoroughly acquainted with the teachings of the ancient mathematicians but also have worked out a new theory about the universe. According to this theory, the earth is in motion and the sun occupies the central position. The eighth sphere (the fixed stars) are fixed motionless in their place; and the moon with everything in its sphere between Mars and Venus rotates around the sun yearly. It is said that you have written up these novel theories, calculated the movements of the planets, and collated all this in tabular form; and that it has had an astonishing impact.
>
> Without wishing to inconvenience you, I would urge you to communicate your findings to the scholarly world, and to send me your theories and tables and related materials. . . .
>
> If you do me this favor, you will soon find out that I have your interests at heart, and that I want you to have the honor you so richly deserve.
>
> With every best wish,
> Rome, November 1, 1536

Despite these words of encouragement, Copernicus kept his theories from publication for another six years. The only explanation is that he himself was not yet sure of them. Even more important, however, Copernicus had no desire to start a revolution. He had no burning ambition to topple the prevailing world view, or to carry out some great mission. In fact, he may not have been fully convinced that his own arguments were foolproof.

We now know that his proofs were in fact inadequate. His theory was still insufficiently supported by valid argument. Copernicus did not know what every schoolchild today knows: that the planetary orbits result from the interaction of

24. Using the Jacob's staff. Left: Astronomer measuring the distance between a star and the moon. Right: measuring the distance to a building whose height is known. Center: measuring the height and distance of a building from the two ends of a measuring line.

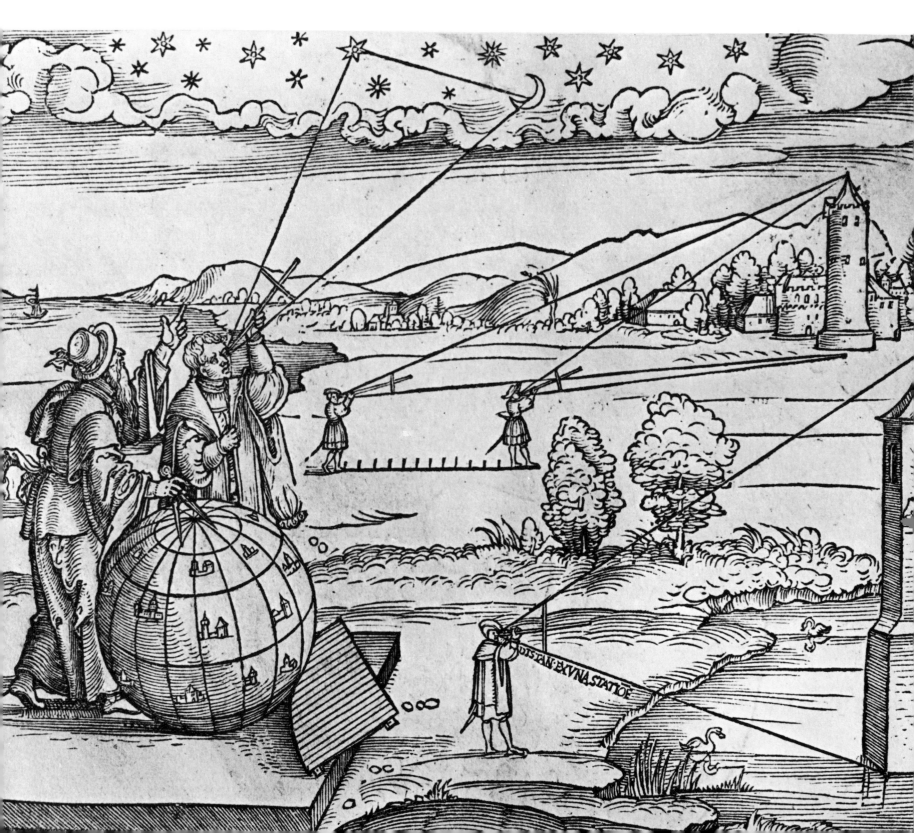

COPERNICUS: THE END OF THE GEOCENTRIC UNIVERSE

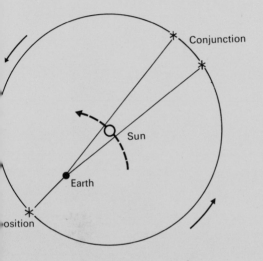

...osition and Conjunction of a superior planet.

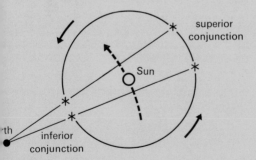

...erior and inferior conjunction of an inferior planet; ...e there is no opposition.

Copernicus stands at the end of a era in astronomy. Three postulates characterize that era: 1) There are five planets: Mercury, Venus, Mars, Jupiter, and Saturn; along with the sun and moon, they have their own characteristic pattern of motion over against the fixed stars. 2) Most scholars of that era operated on the basic assumption that the earth was the center of the universe, hence the center around which the planets moved. 3) A further assumption was that only circular, uniform motion was appropriate for these perfect heavenly bodies.

THE GEOCENTRIC VIEW

Ancient astronomy was dominated by this geocentric outlook. All heavenly phenomena were viewed from earth, the motionless center around which everything revolved. Both motion and rest were relative in terms of the earth itself. As the Greeks saw it, the fixed stars were riveted on a spherical cover. If an observer on earth looked southward, this whole realm of fixed stars appeared to move *uniformly* to the right: that is, from east to west. By close observation, the position of a star could be pinpointed within a system of co-ordinates (see page 186). That point will not be discussed here.

The important point here is that the sun, the moon, and the planets were projected against this backdrop of fixed stars. To an earthly observer, they seemed to be caught up in the motion of the fixed stars also; for they always remained within the zodiac belt, with its twelve "signs" or constellations. Upon closer observation, people noticed that this daily movement of planets, sun, moon, and fixed stars was not the only motion. The sun, moon, and planets also had their own peculiar pattern of motion over against the fixed stars. It took the sun one year to complete its normal course leftward through all the signs of the zodiac. The moon completed this same course in one month.

The situation was slightly more complicated in the case of the planets. Mars, Jupiter, and Saturn usually pursued the normal course *leftward;* but for a brief time they moved in the *opposite* direction, to the *right*. When these successive positions were recorded on a star chart, there was a noticeable looping effect. These loops were repeated during each synodical revolution — i.e. when the planet, as viewed from earth, came directly into the path of the sun. When the earth stood between the planet and the sun, the planet was said to be in opposition to the sun; it then could be seen at midnight. When the planet stood directly in line with the sun, unobstructed by the earth, it was in conjunction with the sun; it could not be seen at all. In terms of the moon, opposition occurred with the full moon, and conjunction with the new moon.

Mercury and Venus also followed a normal pattern of motion, but they never moved far away from the sun. Sometimes they moved ahead of the sun, however, and sometimes they followed it. This movement, called "easterly and westerly elongation," could only be explained by alternating forward and backward motion. No opposition occurred with these "superior" planets, because their orbits lay closer to the sun than that of earth.

ECCENTRIC CIRCLES AND EPICYCLES

How could one explain the complicated motion of the sun, the moon, and the planets, while maintaining that the earth was the center of the universe and that the motion was circular and uniform? The Greek astronomer Hipparchus (c. 190–125 B.C.) formulated a theory of solar and lunar motion which became the basis of Ptolemy's geocentric theory.

Hipparchus noted that the seasons had varying lengths. Spring lasted 92 days, summer 94 days, autumn 89 days, and winter 90 days. He therefore concluded that the sun could not possibly move at a uniform speed in its orbit, unless the midpoint of its orbit did not coincide with the midpoint of the central body in the universe — the earth. So he postulated two distinct orbital points: one near the earth and one distant from the earth. Since its orbit was eccentric to the earth, the sun did seem to go faster when it was near the earth and slower when it was far away from the earth.

The motion of the moon was a more complicated problem. There were many inequalities to be explained, and Hipparchus did formulate a theory. But it was Ptolemy (c. 127–151 A.D.) who added the finishing touches to the theory by introducing the notion of epicycles.

Long before Ptolemy's day, Apollonius (c. 200 B.C.) had put forward the notion that the irregular motion of a heavenly body around a given point could be represented as a *combination* of uniform circular motions. The heavenly body was oriented on a subsidiary orbit, an epicycle; and it moved around this orbit at uniform speed. At the same time, the center of the epicycle moved at uniform speed in another circle (deferent) around a center point. The diagram to the right depicts this view.

Unlike the sun, therefore, the planets did not move in a great circle around the earth; only the center of their epicycles did that. Thus their movement around the earth could easily be explained by the velocity of their arcs and the ratio between the radii of the two circles. Ptolemy assigned values for these factors and thus solved the problem of planetary motion to his own satisfaction.

But the epicycle theory had further advantages. It explained the looping effect in the planetary orbits, and it enabled Ptolemy to chart the position of the various

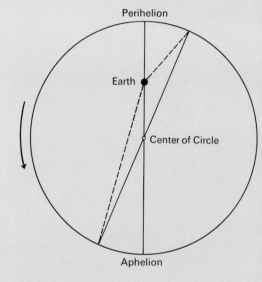

Hipparchus's theory: an orbit eccentric to that of earth.

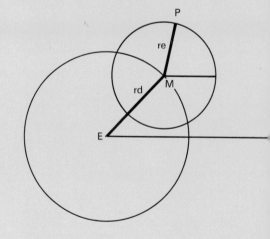

The epicycle theory: planet (P) moves around the earth (E). The circle around the earth with the radius (rd) is the deferent; the circle around midpoint (M) with the radius (re) is the epicycle.

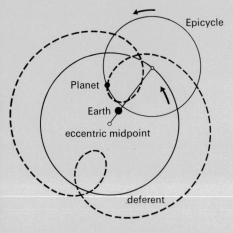

The looping effect according to the epicycle theory

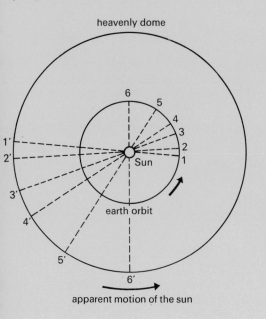

The apparent motion of the sun in the system of Copernicus

heavenly dome

earth orbit

Sun

apparent motion of the sun

bodies from earth outward: the moon, Mercury, and Venus (because of their limited pendular motion around the sun), the sun, Mars, Jupiter, and Saturn. Ptolemy could not give figures for these distances, and he was not particularly interested in that problem. His chief concern was to describe accurately the motion of the sun, the moon, and the planets. By coordinating various cyclic motions with one another, he was able to provide an explanation that satisfied many. Later astronomers added more circles and epicycles when their data seemed to call for them.

THREE BASIC AXIOMS

Copernicus studied the classical literature in the field of astronomy. He then asked himself this question: How could one explain planetary motion if one operated on the assumption that the earth itself, like the other planets, moved around the sun? He soon discovered this assumption provided a simple explanation for the motions of the planets. His theory can be summed up in three basic axioms:

1. The earth makes one full rotation on its axis every day, turning from west to east. Thus the observer on earth sees the heavenly stars apparently moving from east to west.

2. In a year, the earth makes one revolution around the sun, moving from west to east. The sun is at rest in space, its apparent motion being a reflection of the earth's motion.

3. All the planets revolve around the sun just as the earth does. The complex looping effects and elongations result from the fact that their orbiting occurs at different times and at different velocities.

By making the earth like all the other planets and by placing the sun at the center of this system, Copernicus radically challenged the pervading view. His universe was *heliocentric,* not *geocentric.* Yet Copernicus did not break with all the assumptions of classical astronomy. He still accepted the notions of uniform motion and circular orbits. Thus he still had to play around with eccentric circles and epicycles, though he put less stress on them. It was Kepler who eliminated the need for these tricks by proving that the planets moved irregularly in elliptical orbits (see page 5*).

PROOFS FOR HIS THEORY

Let us look briefly at the proofs which Copernicus offered for his theory of a heliocentric universe (see also pages 37 ff.). Copernicus could only talk in terms of probability and plausibility when he spoke of the earth's daily and yearly motion. Was it likely that the fixed stars moved around the earth at some fantastic speed if the same phenomenon could be produced by the relatively minute rotation of the earth itself? Moreover, one would no longer have to explain the mysterious mechanism which caught up the planets in the movement of the fixed stars.

3*

Copernicus also pointed out that if the earth did revolve yearly around the sun, the stars would make slight but systematic shifts of location in the heavens during the year. These shifts would show up when an observer took bearings on the stars from two opposite points in the earth's orbit. Here was a real chance to check his theory, but the opportunity could not be seized at the time. These stellar shifts are so small that they could not be measured accurately with the existing instruments. That is one reason why Tycho Brahe remained sceptical about the heliocentric system (see pages 48 and 8*).

Thus Copernicus could only appeal to the plausibility of his first two axioms. It was really the third axiom that showed the theoretical superiority of the new theory. The observable motions of the other planets, as seen from earth, are readily explainable if their rates of speed are different from that of earth.

An example from everyday life will make this clear. When we are traveling in a car, we may catch sight of a slower car ahead of us. Gradually we catch up to it, run alongside it for a moment, and then watch it fall behind us. Well, this is precisely what happens as the earth overtakes a superior planet (Mars, Jupiter, Saturn), whose orbit is outside that of the earth. The apparent reversal of direction is simply accounted for. By the same token, the motion of an inferior planet (Mercury and Venus), whose orbit is inside that of earth, is akin to what happens when our automobile is overtaken by a faster car on the road.

Thus the motion of a planet is clockwise and forward, if the lines connecting co-ordinate points on its orbit and the earth's orbit, intersect between that planet and earth. Its motion is backward and counterclockwise, if these same lines intersect outside the outer planet: earth, if it is an inferior planet; itself, if it is a superior planet (see diagram). These lines may also run parallel to each other, in which case the planet seems to be stationary.

This explanation of planetary motion could be shored up by Copernicus because he had at his disposal figures from the epicycle theory to indicate the proper solar setup. The sun was surrounded by Mercury and Venus (inferior planets), earth, and the superior planets (Mars, Jupiter, and Saturn).

On the basis of his axioms, Copernicus attempted to work out predictive calculations about the positions of the planets. These calculations, published by his pupil Erasmus Reinhold, represented no improvement over the geocentric system. The two theories were equal on this score. Today we know why. To begin with, the observations were too inexact. Secondly, Copernicus still believed that the planetary orbits were circular.

The breakthrough came when Tycho Brahe provided exact measurements of planetary positions. Using these measurements, Kepler was able to conclude that the planets followed an elliptical orbit at irregular rates of speed.

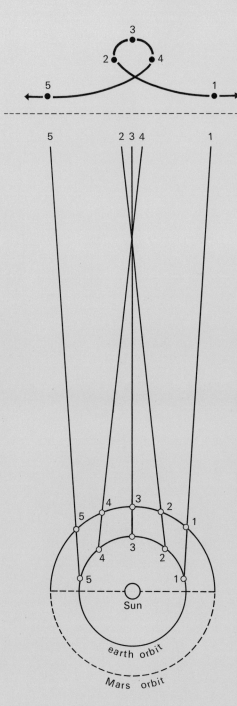

Explanation of the looping effect in the Copernican system.

the gravitational forces of the planets, and that they are not circular but elliptical. He did not possess the data of physics which would have given coherence to his cosmos. The contending forces of scholasticism, humanism, and natural science were at war within him. We can well understand his melancholy deathbed remarks: "The shortness of life, the frailness of reason, and the dull routine of senseless activity do not allow us to gain much knowledge. And what we do learn, we all too soon forget."

His courage and his vision do shine through his work. At times it reads like an ancient hymn to the sun. His vision of a harmonious cosmos seems to be reflected in his own well-ordered life: "It is in the very center of all the planets that the sun finds its place. What better place to set it in this cosmic temple than in the center, where it can shed its light equally on all? Ensconced on its royal throne, it rules over the family of the stars."

5. *Astronomer and student. Woodcut.*

6. *Theologian and astronomer. Woodcut.*

FROM COPERNICUS TO KEPLER

Because of Copernicus's reserved attitude, his ideas did not take root until fifty years after his death. The result was not what he himself would have wanted.

In the interval political events dominated the picture. The Reformation spread through Europe, and the Counter-Reformation gradually took shape. Copernicus had disapproved of this fratricidal war, but it was not to be avoided. The spirit of Erasmus, counseling reform from within the Church, grew fainter and fainter.

When the Protestant princes formed the Schmalkaldic League in 1531, they signaled the end of the medieval political ideal. The Holy Roman Empire would be no more. Christendom would become a complex of national states, ruled by independent sovereigns. In 1534 Henry VIII rejected the authority of the Bishop of Rome over the English Church. That same year, Ignatius of Loyola founded the Society of Jesus, whose main task was to counter the effects of the Reformation.

In 1545, two years after Copernicus's death, the Council of Trent began. It was to last until 1563, introducing reforms into the Catholic Church. As yet there had been no real objections to the Copernican theory, because the Church did not yet regard it as a threat to her teaching. The *De Revolutionibus* was not widely read, and the first edition never sold out. In 1566 a second edition was published in Basle; a third came out in Amsterdam in 1617. Only in 1616 was it put on the Index of forbidden books.

27. *Ignatius of Loyola.*
Engraving (1621) by Lucas Vorstermann,
from a painting by Peter Paul Rubens.

Supported by the Hapsburgs, the Church gained political leverage again through the Council of Trent. But Protestantism had won many successes — in Switzerland, Scandinavia, Scotland, England, the Baltic countries, and parts of Holland. Protestant minorities also appeared in Poland, Hungary and Transylvania. In 1562 the religious war with the Huguenots broke out in France; a struggle for independence broke out in Holland in 1568. Both conflagrations were to last for decades.

There were few major scientific contributions during these war-torn years. The Jesuits began to play an important role in the development of scientific thought. The Order grew rapidly, spreading to all parts of the newly discovered world. Jesuit missionaries established colonies in Japan, China, India, the Philippines, Canada, Mexico, Peru, the Congo, and elsewhere. Open-mindedness to the world mellowed the counter-reformationist outlook of the Order, and made it the leading proponent of modern thought within the Church.

The Jesuits strove to free themselves from the medieval outlook. Their interest in astronomy also had a sound pragmatic basis: the ability to forecast celestial phenomena made a deep impression on alien peoples. This seems to have been the

28. *Admiral Coligny, leader of the Huguenots, is murdered in the Saint Bartholomew's Day Massacre. Engraving (1619).*

29. *Bishops and their theological advisers in session at the Council of Trent.*

30. *The Spanish Armada is defeated by the British in the English Channel. Engraving from the "Historical Chronicle" of 1619.*

case in China, where Jesuits were appointed to work on the reform of the Chinese calendar.

During this period Europe fell back into the clutches of superstition. The persecution of witches reached its high point, and thousands of hapless women were burned at the stake by Protestants and Catholics alike. Many people took a serious interest in alchemy, hunting in vain for the philosopher's stone and the elixir of life. This superstitious hysteria prevailed over the next hundred years.

The most famous heretic of this period was Giordano Bruno, a monk, who was burned at the stake in Rome (1600) for taking the Copernican theory seriously. He had read the works of Copernicus and Nicholas of Cusa, and although he was a religious mystic at heart, he drew some practical conclusions from his reading. The sun floated in space, encircled by the planets. Like the earth, the other planets were inhabited by living beings. God himself is the Mind of the Universe, and we honor him best by investigating the laws of nature. Bruno did not make any concrete contribution to astronomy, but he gave his life in the defense of freedom of thought.

TYCHO BRAHE'S NEW STAR

It was during this interim period that the Danish astronomer, Tycho Brahe, made his contribution to scientific progress. He served as the connecting link between Copernicus and later scientists. Convinced of the importance of empirical investigation, Tycho was the first to stress exact and continuous observation of the heavenly bodies. Tycho was not a disciple of Copernicus, but his many careful observations helped to prove the Copernican theory. While Copernicus made only about seventy direct observations, Tycho made several thousand; and they were far more exact than any made before him.

31. *On August 8, 1576, the foundation was laid for the Uranieborg observatory on the island of Hven. The observation platforms were located under the removable roofs of the spires. In 1584 a new observatory, Stjarneborg, had to be added (see picture below). It housed five observation platforms, situated below ground level for the protection of the instruments. The domed roof-coverings were removable.*

Born on December 14, 1546, this son of a rich nobleman took up astronomy at the age of fourteen. As a student, he fought a duel with a classmate over who was the best mathematician. At the age of sixteen he was sent to Leipzig, and he pursued his studies at the universities of Wittenberg, Rostock, Basle, and Augsburg until he was twenty-six. He bought the best astronomical instruments available, and designed new ones of his own.

On November 11, 1572, Tycho made a discovery that was to make him the talk of Europe: he discovered a new star in the constellation of Cassiopeia. It was a fixed star, shining brighter than Venus, and visible to the naked eye even during the daytime. Europe was aghast. If it could be proved that this was a new fixed star, then the old notion of an unchanging realm of fixed stars would have to be abandoned.

Tycho set out to prove it was a fixed star. His high quality instruments enabled him to make exact measurements. One year later he published his book, *De nova stella,* in which he presented proof for his theory. Tycho could not say how the new star had come into being: it is only in the twentieth century that physics has been able to enlighten us on the origins of *supernovae*. But his careful measurements were

good enough to topple the cosmology of antiquity. The fixed stars were now enmeshed in the process of change.

Tycho was now a famous man. He traveled widely and was often away from his homeland. In 1576 King Frederick II of Denmark sent a courier to entice him back with a fantastic offer. He would receive a handsome yearly pension and a three-mile-long island off Copenhagen. This island would become his property, and on it he could build an observatory at government expense. No astronomer had ever received such an offer before.

So Tycho began to build his observatory, Uraniebörg, on the isle of Hven. His own lodgings were fit for a prince, and his instruments were housed in a tower whose roof could be turned to facilitate observations. Tycho also had his own paper mill and printing press. He lived like the lord of the manor, and received visits from scholars, noblemen, and kings. The palace was filled with mechanical instruments and devices that astounded his guests. There was even a court jester to amuse the renowned astronomer. The peasants on the island had to pay tribute each year. He fell in love with a peasant girl who bore him eight children, but he never condescended to legitimize their union.

For twenty years Tycho Brahe ruled Hven as an absolute monarch, but eventually his insolence brought him into conflict with the young King Christian IV of Denmark. His pension was cut down and he left Denmark in protest. But he took with him his library, his printing press, his instruments, much of his furniture, and a large number of his servants.

After traveling around for two years, he arrived at the court of Rudolf II in Prague (June 1599). Rudolf promised him a castle and an annual income of three thousand guilders—far more than anyone else at his court received. But Tycho soon found out that the impoverished Rudolf could not meet his agreement. He spent so much time trying to get his money that he had little time left over for work. His heavy eating and drinking proved to be his undoing, and he died on October 13, 1601. The scientific importance of his stay in Prague was that while there he met the young Johannes Kepler. Kepler came to Prague in 1600 and eventually fell heir to Tycho's post.

32. Tycho Brahe observing the stars with the help of his large wall quadrants. With the aid of three assistants, he is calculating the zenith and declination of the stars. In the foreground are two clocks, which were regarded as quite accurate by his contemporaries. Tycho is pointing to a hole in the wall, through which he makes his celestial observations.

IOANNIS KEPPLERI
Mathematici Cæsarei
hanc Imaginem

ARGENTORATENSI BIBLIOTHECÆ
Confecr.

MATTHIAS BERNEGGERVS
kal. Ianuar. Anno Chr.
M DC. XXVII

JOHANNES KEPLER

Born: December 27, 1571, in Weil der Stadt

Died: November 15, 1630, in Regensburg

"MY PURPOSE IS TO DEMONSTRATE THAT THE HEAVENLY BODIES ARE NOT LIVING DIVINE BEINGS BUT A COMPLEX PIECE OF CLOCKWORK: THAT THEIR VARIOUS MOVEMENTS ARE GOVERNED BY A MAGNETIC AND MATERIAL FORCE, JUST AS THE MOVEMENTS OF A CLOCK ARE GOVERNED BY A SIMPLE WEIGHT."

Letter of Johannes Kepler (c. 1605)

The previous page shows a portrait of Kepler from the Regensburg Municipal Collection.

Right: At the age of 23, Kepler accidentally embarked on what was to be his chosen career. The young theology student became a mathematics teacher in Graz in order to support himself. He received an annual stipend of 150 guilders, made his first calculations, and used astronomical instruments for the first time. The small angular devise is a portable sun dial.

Left: For a long time Kepler had no telescope with which to verify his observations about Jupiter's satellites. Galileo ignored his persistent requests for a telescope. Finally, a wealthy amateur astronomer lent him his telescope while he was passing through Prague. On the desk is a first edition of Copernicus's "De revolutionibus", with Tycho Brahe's notes pencilled in. There is also Tycho Brahe's stellar-planetary catalogue with Kepler's own corrections.

Next page (left): In Prague Kepler became Tycho's assistant. Rudolf II gave Tycho a small castle to be used as an observatory. From the terrace Kepler observed Mars with the instruments he had ordered from Dresden. For six years Kepler observed the heavens, and he filled 900 pages with his calculations. He was finally led to realize that the planetary orbits must be elliptical.

Next page (right): Kepler succeeded Tycho Brahe as Rudolf II's court astronomer. On the table is a copy of his "Astronomia Nova," with a picture of Rudolf II on the title page. Near the entrance is another portrait of Rudolf II.

Previous page: A seventeenth-century (1600–1617) depiction of the planetary orbits, in the Munich planetarium. The loops are plainly seen. It was these loops that puzzled ancient and medieval astronomers. Only by placing the sun at the center of the planetary system and downgrading the earth were astronomers able to abandon the epicycle theory and explain the loops.

Below: All torture chambers in Germany were built according to a standard design. The last such chamber is still intact in Regensburg.

Right: Kepler's discoveries came in the early days of printing. His most important work, "Harmonice mundi," was printed in Linz. On the typecase are his manuscripts.

THE PIONEER OF
SCIENTIFIC THOUGHT

Previous double page: When Emperor Matthias moved to Regensburg, he brought his astronomer with him as Matthias was anxious to demonstrate the superiority of the Gregorian calendar over the Julian calendar. The Protestant princes viewed the Gregorian calendar with suspicion and distrust, regarding it as a papal deceit. For another hundred years both calendars were recognized.

Left: Kepler spent his last years in Regensburg, where he died on November 15, 1630. In his quarters we find his work desk, the last celestial globe he used, and his own inventory of his personal possessions.

The fierce acceleration at takeoff is the worst, for the traveler will feel as if he had been shot from a cannon. He must be anesthetized in some way, and his limbs must be carefully protected lest they be torn apart. Soon he will face new problems: the temperature will become fiercely cold, and breathing will be difficult. Once the first stage of the journey is over, it will be easier. His body will escape the magnetic force of the earth and come under that of the moon, as the latter gradually gains the upper hand. At this point the traveler will be set free and left to his own devices. His limbs will expand and contract, and they will move about like spiders. The magnetic force of the earth and the moon will balance out, so that the travelers will be suspended between them. Eventually their body mass will turn to the moon of its own accord.

Johannes Kepler had this dream of space travel even as a young student. He worked over it for many years and eventually wrote a book about it. It was the first science-fiction story, and his description of life on the moon was nightmarish. The moon dwellers, for example, resembled prehistoric reptiles. When we read his description of physical conditions on the moon, however, we feel that we are reading a modern work. The dark side of the moon is a frozen expanse of ice and snow. By contrast, the bright side of the moon has a temperature that is fifteen times higher than that of Africa. Imaginary visions and concrete physical data are curiously intermixed.

Kepler was not frightened by the newly discovered universe or by the insignificance of the planet earth. He was the first astronomer to take the Copernican theory seriously. Galileo Galilei, seven years older and already more famous, did not come out in support of the theory until later. When he did, he claimed that he had been a proponent of the theory for a long time. But he taught the Ptolemaic system for decades, while Kepler defended the Copernican theory even as a young student.

THE FAULTFINDING MATHEMATICIAN

Johannes Kepler was born in Weil der Stadt (Württemberg) on December 27, 1571. He was born of nobility, since his grandfather had been made a knight by the emperor, but he grew up in poverty. He remained a poor astronomer all his life. Money problems vexed him continually, sickness dogged his tracks, and fortune dealt harshly with him.

At twenty-six he described himself harshly as a "dog-faced" creature. He held similarly harsh views about those around him, particularly his close relatives. His father was a "malicious, quarrelsome, stubborn man who would come to a bad end." In his pursuit of fame and fortune, his father ran the risk of being hanged, maltreated his wife, and eventually left the country. His mother, who was later indicted as a witch, was a "small, thin woman given to gossip and quarreling."

Kepler's critical eye was matched by his interest in learning. He faced up to any assignment, no matter how difficult it was. He wrote poetry, read Aristotle in the original Greek, espoused the doctrine of predestination, and accepted Luther's view on the absence of free will. Later he attacked this latter view. Though he was a theology student, his favorite subject was mathematics. So it was that his teacher and lifelong friend, Michael Mästlin, recommended the twenty-three-year-old student for the post of mathematics teacher at the Protestant school in Graz.

The young teacher arrived in Graz in April 1594. He had few pupils in his first year and none in his second. His superiors wanted him to earn his pay, so they let him teach rhetoric as well. His other duties included the task of drawing up a calendar each year and adding astrological predictions to it. Thanks to his sceptical bent, he was able to glimpse the right turn of events. His dire predictions about Turkish invasion and severe winter weather came true.

Kepler himself viewed astrology with grave misgivings, and called it "the stepdaughter of astronomy". Although he never rejected it entirely, he did not believe in the possibility of pinpoint prophesying. But his successful predictions stood him in good stead, adding to his prestige and winning him promotion.

33. Title page of Kepler's calendar for the year 1598.

GEOMETRY AND THE HEAVENS

In Linz, Kepler worked away on his first astronomy book, *Mysterium Cosmographicum*. The full title of the book suggests that it is "a pioneer work in cosmography, revealing the mysterious and wondrous proportions between the celestial orbits and the authentic natural basis for their number, size, and periodic movements." Kepler wanted to unveil the mystery of the planetary orbits, to pick up Copernicus's inquiry into the harmonious order of the universe. On July 19, 1595, he had a sudden flash of insight: the six planetary orbits are ordered in a geometric series, patterned after Plato's perfect shapes — the tetrahedron, the hexahedron (or cube), the octahedron, the dodecahedron, and the icosahedron.

Kepler decided to tie in the space between the planets with the five polyhedra, and he believed that he had found a plausible scheme. Between Saturn and Jupiter he positioned a cube; between Jupiter and Mars, a tetrahedron; between Mars and earth, a dodecahedron; between earth and Venus, an icosahedron; between Venus and Mercury, an octahedron. In the center, of course, was the ball-shaped sun.

For his whole life Kepler held on to this model scheme, which was esthetically satisfying but hardly demonstrable. He honestly believed he had solved the riddle of the universe with this geometric scheme. Geometry, indeed, was God: "Geometry

34. The five solid figures, or polyhedra. On account of the importance Plato accorded them in his own thinking, they are also known as the five Platonic solids. One of their characteristics was particularly interesting to Kepler: all five could be inscribed within a circle. In other words, all the corners of a polyhedron lie on a tangent plane. Since six planets, including earth, were known in Kepler's day, the five Platonic polyhedra could be situated between the spherical orbits in which the planets were thought to move.

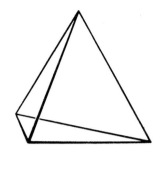

Tetrahedron

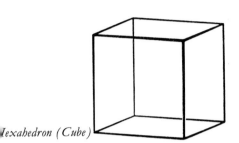

Hexahedron (Cube)

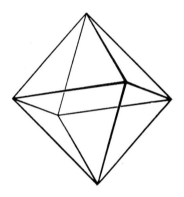

Octahedron

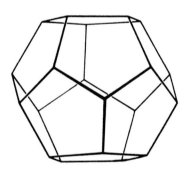

Dodecahedron

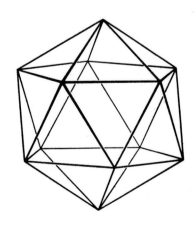

Icosahedron

existed before creation, eternal like the Spirit of God. Geometry indeed is God himself. It provided him with a ready model for creation, and it was implanted in man along with God's image." The important point, however, is that this geometric model enabled Kepler to make further important discoveries. Working with this model, Kepler discovered the three laws of planetary motion which gave strong support to the Copernican theory.

When Kepler completed this book in 1597, he married. It was a marriage of convenience, and love played little part in his decision. As soon as his book was printed, Kepler sent a copy to a fellow professor of mathematics, Galileo Galilei. Despite their common interests, there was an important difference between them. The twenty-six-year-old mathematics professor in Graz was a poor man; the thirty-three-year-old professor in Padua was the favored protégé of eminent people.

Kepler received a rather noncommittal letter from Galileo, but one point in it is noteworthy. Galileo said that he had espoused the Copernican theory for some years, but that he was afraid to defend it openly for fear of ridicule. On October 13, 1597, a friend of Kepler was setting out for Italy, and Kepler used the opportunity to send a reply to Galileo. He urged him to publicize his discoveries and the Copernican theory. By standing up for the truth, he would help himself and his colleagues in this matter: "You can help your beleaguered colleagues with the comfort of your support and the backing of your prestige. It is not only the Italians who refuse to believe that they and the earth are in motion. That notion is not popular here in Germany either."

In his note Kepler also told Galileo that he had no decent instruments, and he asked his Italian colleague to make certain observations for him. They concerned his presumption about movement in the fixed stars, proof of which would lend support to the notion that the earth itself moved. Galileo did not answer Kepler's note, nor did he do what Kepler asked. Twelve years passed before Kepler received another letter from Galileo.

KEPLER AND TYCHO BRAHE

Kepler sent another copy of his book to Tycho Brahe, who was very favorably impressed by it. Although he did not accept Kepler's celestial geometry, he glimpsed the original genius behind these ideas. But Kepler did not fare much better at Tycho's hands. His dream of working with the Danish astronomer still remained unfulfilled. Moreover, Tycho would not publicize his own observations because he had not yet fully worked out his own system; and he held on to his instruments tenaciously. Any one of these instruments cost more than Kepler and his family could afford. So Kepler came to a decision: "I shall have to try to wrest them away from him." With this intention he set out for Prague in 1600.

Kepler was the first scientific scholar to champion the Copernican theory openly. The Tychonic system (see page 15) did not interest him, because he regarded it as an untenable compromise between the Ptolemaic system and the Copernican system.

But Kepler did want Tycho's carefully guarded findings and his superb instruments. The underlying reason for Kepler's decision, however, was a feeling of desperation. For all his interest in visiting Tycho Brahe and using his instruments, he was motivated primarily by his own precarious position in Graz. The Archduke Ferdinand, who had been a pupil of the Jesuits and who was later to become Emperor Ferdinand II, had begun to expel Protestants from Graz. Kepler's school was closed down in 1598, and all the Protestant teachers were burned at the stake. Only Kepler was able to return with immunity, because he was in favor with the Jesuits. But he did not feel truly safe.

In August 1599, Tycho Brahe procured a castle near Prague, which he intended to convert into a second Uraniebörg. The construction work began, but it soon ran into difficulties. The emperor could not provide the finances he had promised, some of Tycho's assistants had not arrived, and many of the instruments were not yet in Prague. Intrigue and petty jealousies marred the work atmosphere. Moreover, the plague had broken out and there was great danger of contagion.

That was the situation when Kepler arrived. The contrast between the rich Tycho Brahe and himself could not have been more striking, but they shared the same irascible temperament. Each sought to use the other for his own purposes, and an air of antagonism soon developed. Tycho would not let Kepler use his instruments or read his findings. But he assigned him the most difficult task: calculating the orbit of Mars. Tycho and his chief assistant, Longomontanus, had been unsuccessful in trying to solve that problem.

The real source of the difficulty was that the orbit of Mars is far more sharply elliptical than those of the other planets. This fact was unknown at the time. Mars had been the despair of astronomers because they assumed that all the planets moved in circular orbits. Thus they could not coordinate their observatory findings with their calculations.

Tycho now assigned this problem to Kepler, but he did not put his own findings at Kepler's disposal. Kepler got no further with the problem, and Mars became his star of fate. Neither was Tycho willing to guarantee financial security to Kepler. Within a month they had a heated argument, and Kepler stormed out of the castle. But a few weeks later Tycho went to see Kepler in Prague and brought him back to the castle with him. He probably had come to realize what a valuable find Kepler was.

When Kepler left later to clear up family matters, Tycho wrote him a friendly letter. He told Kepler to return as soon as he could, and to put his trust in him. The emperor had confirmed Kepler's appointment. Kepler now brought his wife to Prague, and Tycho, at the request of the emperor, transferred his headquarters there. Kepler made one more trip to Graz, trying to claim the estate left by his rich father-in-law. His efforts were unsuccessful. But two months after he returned to Prague, Tycho died; Kepler was promptly installed as the imperial mathematician. He was free at last, or so he thought.

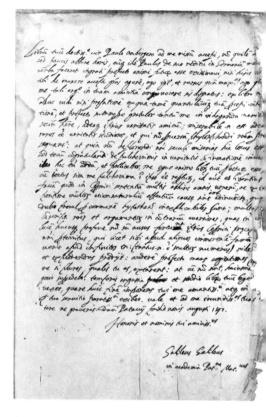

35. *Letter of Galileo to Kepler, dated August 4, 1597. In it Galileo openly espouses the Copernican theory.*

36. *Emperor Rudolf II. Engraving, after a painting by Johann von Aachen.*

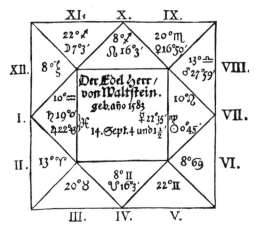

37. Kepler's horoscope for Wallenstein.

38. Albrecht von Wallenstein, Duke of Friedland.
Contemporary engraving by Peter Isselburg.

Kepler remained in Prague until the death of Rudolf II in 1612. His most important achievements came during this period, but he had to fight hard for them. For a whole year he had to contend with Tycho's former dependants, who sought to take possession of his instruments and calculations.

Kepler also had a wide range of duties as the imperial mathematician. Here, too, he had to work up astrological calendars and horoscopes. One of the horoscopes became famous. Prepared for a young general named Wallenstein, it accurately plotted the future course of his career.

Kepler spent three years writing his major work, *Astronomia nova (New Astronomy)*. It was finished around Easter in 1605, but publication was delayed by litigation with Tycho's heirs. In the book Kepler had expropriated Tycho's sketches.

While all this was going on, Kepler proceeded to write a book about a new star that had appeared in 1604. To this day the star is known as "Kepler's nova." As Tycho had done before him, Kepler proved that his new star belonged to the realm of the fixed stars and thus cast further doubt on the immutability of the fixed stars. In 1604 Kepler also published a book on optics, setting forth the basic principles for the use of optical instruments and anticipating the use of the telescope. It was not until 1610 that Galileo became the first man to look at the stars through a telescope.

During this same period, Galileo was still preoccupied with the laws of falling bodies and the laws of pendular motion. Kepler, on the other hand, was to uncover the first two laws of planetary motion (see p. 75).

Kepler actually discovered the second law before he discovered the first, and he caught a glimpse of the third law in one of his earliest works. Without knowing that the planetary orbits are elliptical rather than circular, he rightly concluded that the speed of rotation around the sun was not the same for all the planets. The third law is hinted at in his first work, where he tries to describe in mathematical terms the relationship between the revolution of a planet and its distance from the sun. The first thing he realized was that the outer planets move more slowly than the inner planets, and that the difference between their movement was absolute not relative. Saturn, for example, was twice as far away from the sun as Jupiter, but it took two and a half times as long to circle the sun. There had to be some force responsible for this, and Kepler imagined it had to be in the sun. He was the first to look for physical causes behind the motions of the planets.

The second law resulted from Kepler's work with the planet Mars. Mars was Kepler's nemesis and his helpmate as well. The bane of astronomers, it remained a puzzle for centuries. Gradually, Kepler came to realize that the irregular revolution of Mars must have resulted from the fact that two opposing forces are at work: one force deriving from the sun, the other force from the planet itself. That was why the planet first moved closer to the sun and then moved away from it again.

The first law came later. Kepler could not pinpoint the orbit of Mars. He was still under the impression that the planetary orbits were circular. Years later, in the fourth book of his *Astronomia nova,* he came to the important conclusion that the planetary orbits could not be circular. He asserted that they were oval in shape. But he did not have the courage to maintain this position, so he again rejected his own conclusion. Over a decade later he again came to the notion of an elliptical orbit; but again he rejected his own solution. He started over again; again he arrived at the notion of an elliptical orbit. Then he was willing to admit that the truth he had been seeking so earnestly had been there all the time.

KEPLER AND GALILEO

Kepler's contemporaries were unwilling to follow his lead. The theories of his new astronomy did not find a ready following. Astronomers rejected the theory of elliptical orbits. Neither his teacher, Mästlin, nor the great Galileo recognized its importance.

Kepler's relationship with Galileo was a patchwork affair. Only in 1610 did he again establish direct contact with Galileo, when the latter published his book entitled *Sidereus nuncius* ("Celestial Messenger"). This was Galileo's first scientific work to be published, and he was then forty-six. It bore witness to his observations of the heavens through a telescope. Galileo was the first astronomer to use this instrument; and through its use he discovered that there were mountains and valleys on the moon, that there were countless stars invisible to the naked eye, and that the milky way was an enormous mass of stars. His discovery of four moons around Jupiter created a sensation. Galileo was sure that no man had ever seen them before. But Galileo himself considered them to be planets, not satellite moons.

Galileo had greater success with his book than Copernicus or Kepler had with their works. The immutability of the fixed stars was no longer tenable, the planetary system was cast in a new light, and a whole new world was opened up to human vision.

Kepler was the first to support the notions propounded by Galileo. He had heard reports about the book before it was published, and he waited expectantly for a copy to arrive. Galileo, by contrast, did not respond to Kepler's correspondence; nor did he ever take a position publicly on Kepler's books. Now, however, he asked Kepler to give his opinion of his own book. Kepler hastened to do this, though he had to take a great deal on trust as, having no telescope, he was unable to check any of Galileo's observations.

In eleven days Kepler wrote up his commentary on the book, supporting Galileo's work and praising it as a pioneering effort. A month later, his commentary was published in Prague: a patchwork Italian translation was published in Florence. Then Kepler urgently requested Galileo to send his telescope to Prague, so that he could verify Galileo's discoveries. There was no reply from Galileo. Kepler waited for several months, and then wrote to Galileo again. He told him that comments of Galileo's opponents had reached Prague, insisting that "these planets cannot be seen through your telescope". He implored Galileo to send him the telescope.

39. In his first book (1596) Kepler believed he had solved the riddle of cosmic order and planetary orbiting by the use of Plato's geometric figures.

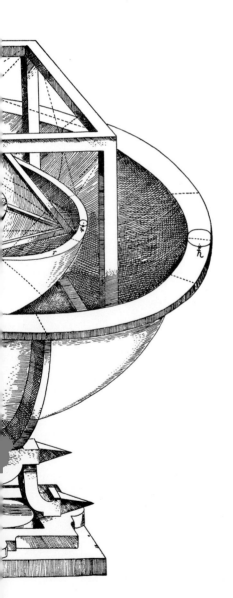

This time Galileo sent a reply. It is his second and last letter to Kepler. Galileo made excuses and chose to sidestep the matter. Again Kepler was left in the lurch. Not once did Galileo give Kepler exact information about his progress. Neither did he tell Kepler that he had just discovered Saturn's rings.

Finally, in the summer of 1610, Kepler managed to borrow a powerful telescope from the Duke of Brunswick. Using it, he was able to see the moons around Jupiter. He sent another letter to Galileo, describing the satellite character of these moons and using the word "satellite" for the first time. Galileo never answered him, nor did he ever publicize Kepler's own discoveries and contributions. He never came to realize that Kepler could provide the theoretical basis which would explain how a telescope worked. Kepler's book on optics (1604) had suggested the possible use of the telescope, and had provided a theoretical basis for the use of eye-glasses. In 1610, he wrote another paper on optics, establishing a new science which he called "dioptics." It was the science of "refracting light through lenses." Kepler was the father of modern optics, and his theory laid the basis for the Keplerian telescope.

AN UNLUCKY YEAR

1612 was an unlucky year. Civil wars were raging, the emperor was forced to abdicate, and diseases ravaged Europe. Kepler's youngest child, his favorite, died of smallpox. Shortly afterwards, his wife of fourteen years, Barbara, also died.

After the death of the emperor on January 20, 1612, Kepler moved to Linz, where he had secured the post of mathematician. It was a demotion for the former imperial mathematician, even though he retained the latter title for life. Shortly after his arrival in Linz, he became involved in a heated theological dispute with the Protestant pastor. Kepler had no intention of being a reformer, and he was an ardent believer. But he could not accept Luther's teaching about the earthly presence of Christ's body. Eventually he was denied participation at the communion table.

In 1615, Kepler's mother, who was living near Weil der Stadt in Leonberg, was accused of being a witch. That same year six women in her village were burned as witches; witch-hunting became the local pastime. Kepler's mother fled to her son in Linz, and then moved on to Württemberg. Kepler followed her, and wrote petitions to the court in her defense. But Kepler himself was now under a cloud because he had dabbled in forbidden arts: he had written a science-fiction novel, *Somnium*, describing a trip to the moon.

The oppression persisted for a long time. On August 5, 1620, his mother was arrested in the rectory of her son-in-law. The bailiffs dragged her to prison in a trunk. At the hearing she denied that she was a witch, and it was decreed that she be put on the rack. Kepler hastened to Württemberg as soon as she was arrested, and he managed to win her a reprieve. For weeks the old woman was confined to prison in chains. She was watched day and night. Kepler fought determinedly, writing paper after paper in her defense and making countless petitions to the court. He managed to save her from torture. She was interrogated under the simple threat of torture, and finally set free a year later. Six months later she died.

THE MATHEMATICIAN AT WORK

Kepler's second marriage was both happy and unhappy. While at Linz, Kepler married Susanne Reutinger in 1613. The twenty-four year-old bride was only a maidservant, and some of Kepler's friends objected to the match. But he married her nevertheless, and she bore him seven children. Four of them survived, as compared to the two out of five of his first marriage.

For the first time, Kepler led a happy domestic life. He was a good husband and father, and he even wrote a booklet for the religious instruction of his children and servants.

Like Luther, Kepler often used the vernacular. He was the first scientist to write

40. Witch burning. Woodcut from a leaflet dated 1555.

KEPLER: THREE LAWS OF PLANETARY MOTION

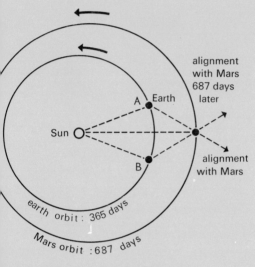

...ler determined the orbit of Mars from two ...ssive observations; the observations were ...rated in time by the length of one complete Mars ...

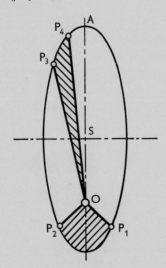

...ler's second law: (S) Sun; (P₁, P₂, P₃, P₄) (S) *Sun;* (P_1, P_2, P_3, P_4)
...ous positions of a planet. The area $(S\ P_1\ P_2)$
...ual to the area $(S\ P_3\ P_4)$*. The planet traverses*
P_2 *and* $P_3\ P_4$ *in equal times.*

Mars was a key factor in the work of Kepler. The motion of this planet was most perplexing to astronomers; in spite of this, or perhaps because of this, Kepler progressed by tackling the problem of Mars.

MARS AND ITS ORBIT

The orbit of Mars was extremely eccentric, and hence the motion of the planet was highly irregular. Anyone who wanted to improve existing planetary theory would have to be able to explain the complicated behavior of Mars. Kepler had two advantages: 1) he possessed Tycho Brahe's careful measurements of Mars' position; 2) he firmly accepted the truth of the heliocentric theory.

Kepler began by deducing the orbit of *earth* from the measurements on Mars. For only when he had worked out the earth's orbit, could he work out the true orbit of other planets observed from the earth. In short, he knew that he would have to take account of the earth's motion in his calculations.

This was a relatively simple task. Kepler could start out with several Mars oppositions observed by Tycho Brahe; the latter observed ten such oppositions between 1580 and 1600. Then, using multiples of its synodical period as his base, Kepler had other observations of Mars at his disposal. Kepler knew that in this case Mars stood at an equivalent, real point in its orbit; alterations in its observed position could *only* be due to alterations in the earth's position vis-à-vis Mars. By repeated calculations, Kepler could extract the influencing factors and gradually plot new positions for earth. The resultant graph indicated that the earth followed an eccentric circle around the sun. The orbit of earth was established.

Using this data, Kepler could now work in the opposite direction to determine the full orbit of Mars. He then set out to find a closed curve that would tie together all the calculated positions of Mars. He tried various spherical shapes, but none of them proved satisfactory. The discrepancy between observation and calculation was at least eight minutes of arc. Since Tycho's measurements were exact within one minute of arc, the calculated orbital shapes could not be correct.

Starting out on a new series of calculations, Kepler decided to use the ellipse as the basic shape. Suddenly theory and observation fitted together neatly. Kepler became fully convinced that the planetary orbits were ellipses, when observations of other planets could be fitted together neatly by postulating similar ellipses with the sun as the common focal point.

Kepler's second law—the radius vector of a planet traverses equal areas of its ellipse in equal times—was also deduced from practical experience. But it provided the explanation for the irregular speed noted by Hipparchus (see page 178). It explained why a planet must move faster when it is nearer to the sun.

The existence of these two laws convinced Kepler that he had come closer to solving the riddle of celestial harmony. Over and over again he sought to integrate into new combinations his calculations and conclusions about planetary ellipses. Again, by chance, he met with success. He considered the mean distance of the planets from the sun, using the earth's mean distance as the base. Then he considered the period of each planet: that is, the time it takes to orbit the sun. Then he began to examine and compare various powers of these figures (square, cube, etc.). After eliminating an error that had slipped into his calculations, he found himself with another planetary law. It is his greatest contribution to planetary theory. It is that the square of a planet's period is equal to the cube of its mean distance from the sun.

Once again Kepler had arrived at a basic law by practical reckoning. He imagined that there was some central force that kept the planets moving around the sun. But is was Newton who discovered the law of gravity and thus pinpointed the basic cause behind all three of Kepler's laws.

Planet	Mean Distance	Period	Distance Cubed	Period Squared
Mercury	0,387	0,241	0,058	0,058
Venus	0,723	0,615	0,378	0,378
Earth	1,000	1,000	1,000	1,000
Mars	1,524	1,881	3,540	3,538
Jupiter	5,203	11,86	140,8	140,66
Saturn	9,539	29,46	868,0	867,9

This chart shows the point of Kepler's third law. The period of the earth and its distance from the sun is arbitrarily set at 1. Note that the square of the period equals the cube of the planet's distance from the sun.

ASTRONOMY'S CRUCIAL PROBLEM

With Kepler we encounter the crucial problem of astronomy and the main difficulties facing astrophysics. Allowing for certain exceptions that have taken on importance in our day, we can say that all information is carried to us here on earth by means of light. Almost everything we know about the building stones of the cosmos has come from the analysis of light waves, waves propagated and emitted by atomic processes in the celestial bodies. (Today we are also getting more and more information from other parts of the spectrum—see page 12*.)

Thus we now operate on the tacit assumption that physical laws are the same everywhere. Astronomy generally proceeds on the hypothesis that physical laws are independent of time and space. In other words, there is no difference between an atom emitting radiation in a laboratory and an atom emitting radiation within a star; and it does not matter whether the light emission took place yesterday or three million years ago.

This hypothesis is basic to all astronomical research, and there seems to be little reason to question it. It has held up well right to the present. Moreover, it has allowed for fruitful collaboration between astronomy and astrophysics. It has shown that certain prevailing conditions—e.g. pressure and temperature—are to be found in the universe, to a degree that could never be reproduced in the laboratory. So true is this that astrophysics is often described as the branch of physics which deals with extreme degrees of pressure and temperature.

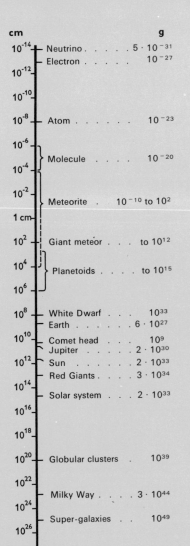

cm		g
10^{-14}	Neutrino	$5 \cdot 10^{-31}$
	Electron	10^{-27}
10^{-12}		
10^{-10}		
10^{-8}	Atom	10^{-23}
10^{-6}		
	Molecule	10^{-20}
10^{-4}		
10^{-2}		
	Meteorite	10^{-10} to 10^2
1 cm		
10^2	Giant meteor	to 10^{12}
10^4	Planetoids	to 10^{15}
10^6		
10^8	White Dwarf	10^{33}
	Earth	$6 \cdot 10^{27}$
10^{10}	Comet head	10^9
	Jupiter	$2 \cdot 10^{30}$
10^{12}	Sun	$2 \cdot 10^{33}$
	Red Giants	$3 \cdot 10^{34}$
10^{14}	Solar system	$2 \cdot 10^{33}$
10^{16}		
10^{18}		
10^{20}	Globular clusters	10^{39}
10^{22}		
	Milky Way	$3 \cdot 10^{44}$
10^{24}	Super-galaxies	10^{49}
10^{26}		
10^{28}	Total universe	10^{55}?

Dimension and mass in the universe. From microcosm to macrocosm the range goes from 1/100 billionth of a centimeter to 10 billion light years. 1 gram = .04 ounces. 1 centimeter = .39 inches

Kepler spent his life exploring the mystery of the structure of the universe; but "universe" to him meant the planetary system. He did not devote his attention to the fixed stars, because he had no way of knowing their constitution or of calculating their distance from the earth.

So let us consider the building blocks of the cosmos for a moment. A "disordered" mass of matter confronts us in interstellar space. It is composed of gas (99%) and dust (1%) which often coagulates into cloud-like configurations. This interstellar matter becomes visible insofar as it dims the light of background stars or is lit up by the radiation from brightly burning stars in the vicinity.

Of the dust matter, the largest elements are the meteorites; their mass may well exceed 100 tons. They are formed either by the coagulation of interplanetary matter (e.g. under the influence of magnetic force fields) or by the breakup of some larger body (e.g. a planet or planetoid). Planetoids, as we have seen (page 139), are small bodies revolving between Mars and Jupiter. The planets are the largest bodies in the solar system which do not emit any light of their own; they merely reflect the light which they receive from the sun.

The next largest building blocks in the cosmos are the fixed stars. They are giant balls of gas, generating their own light, heat, and energy through internal nuclear processes. These stars undergo change and development. Apparently they arise from a conglomeration of interstellar matter. During their lifetime (several billion years) they alter their temperature, size, and chemical makeup in accordance with well-known physical laws. The final stage seems to be a "white dwarf," a star that is smaller than the large planets of our own solar system.

The simplest and most impressive examples of smaller galaxies are the globular star clusters. They comprise several thousand stars, and the distance between the stars in the central regions is comparable with the distance between the planets. At least 200 such clusters are visible in and around our own Milky Way. They are relatively old clusters in astronomical terms, dating back several billion years. The open star clusters, by contrast, are relatively young, dating back several million years; their stars appeared simultaneously.

Like other galaxies, our Milky Way is an aggregation of hundreds of billions of stars. If we examine the distances between the smaller buildings blocks and the galaxies, we come across an interesting fact. The ratio between the diameter of a simple building block and the mean distance of the nearest similar building block is about 1:100 million; but the ratio between galaxies is only 1:10 million. This means that galaxies stay relatively close together; and in fact they often form groups among themselves. Our Milky Way, for example, forms a "local group" with the Magellanic Clouds, the Andromeda nebula, and about twenty other galaxies. This group, in turn, appears to belong to a cluster of supergalaxies.

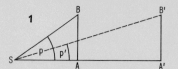

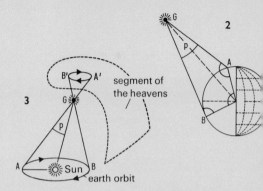

The problem of accurate estimation of distances in the cosmos could only be taken up after the telescope had come on the scene. Only then did man have exact sighting devices which enabled him to measure minute angles. Cosmic measurement involves the measurement of triangles which are very slim because of the enormous distances involved; the critical angles, therefore, are very small.

1. The distance to the sun and moon. The distance between earth and the sun represents a unit of length for astronomy. Various methods, devised by Greek astronomers, led to calculations which we now know were far too small. Ptolemy, for example, put the distance between earth and the sun at 1200 earth radii.

Modern astronomy no longer tries to determine this distance directly. Instead it makes a detour around a small planet that can be observed particularly well from earth and that comes fairly close to earth. It takes sightings of this planet from two points on earth at the same time. From the angles thus obtained, we can calculate the distance in miles. Now Kepler's third law correlates planetary distances with the length of their period. With *one* direct measurement in hand, we can calculate all the others in the solar system. This is one of the ways we can calculate the distance from earth to the sun. The resultant figure, the astronomical unit, is 92,900,000 miles.

The distance to the moon can be measured directly by taking sightings from two points on earth. The mean distance between the center of the earth and that of the moon is 238,866 miles. Interestingly enough, Hipparchus's figure of 59 times the radius of earth is quite close; our modern figure is 60 times the radius of earth.

2. The distance to the fixed stars. To measure the distance to the fixed stars we must find some other base line; for no earthly base will do. The angle would be too small to provide us with an accurate measurement. Here we use the diameter of the earth's orbit as our base line. How is this done? When we judge that a star is relatively close to us, we take bearings on it in the spring and again in the autumn. The earth is at the two extreme points in its orbit in spring and autumn. The resultant angular displacement, which is called the "parallax," enables us to measure the distance involved (see page 4*). F. W. Bessel (1784–1846) was the first astronomer to provide such measurements. Between 1838 and 1840, he determined the parallax of fixed star 61 in Cygnus (the Swan). His figure was 0.37 seconds of arc, a value much too small for Tycho Brahe to have measured. What distance does this parallax represent? Well, a parallax of 1 second of arc represents 19,150,000,000,000 miles. Obviously we are dealing with distances that cannot be expressed practically in miles. As a result, two other units of measurement have been introduced: the light year and the parsec. A light year is the distance traveled by light in one year (at 186,000 miles per second). A parsec is the distance involved in a parallax of 1 second of arc (see table). Looking at the chart on the right, we can compare the distances of several celestial bodies. Light reaches us from the moon in about one second, and from the sun in about eight minutes. From the nearest fixed star, however, the journey takes over four years. The distance to more distant stars and galaxies (see pp. 162–164 and p. 22*) can be deduced from certain optical characteristics.

1. Angle (p), the parallax, becomes smaller, the farther the base (AB) is from (S). (AB = A' B'

2. Determining the parallax (p) of a member of our solar system, using the base (AB) on earth.

3. Determining the "trigonometric or yearly parallax" (p) of a nearby fixed star (G). It is calculated from the apparent positional shift (A' B') of G, which results from the changed sight line (AG or BG) of an observer on earth at different points (A, B) in the earth's orbit. The earth's motion is reflected in A' B'.

Parallax in Angle Seconds	Kilometers	Light Years	Parsec
1	30 871 000 000 000	3,263	1
0,1	308 710 000 000 000	32,63	10
0,01	3 087 100 000 000 000	326,3	100
0,001	30 871 000 000 000 000	3263	1000

The Five Closest Fixed Stars

Name	Parallax	Parsecs	Light years
Alpha in Centaurus	0,760	1,3	4,3
Barnard's Star	0,545	1,8	6,0
Wolf 359	0,421	2,4	7,7
Lalande 21185	0,398	2,5	8,2
Luyten 726–728	0,375	2,6	8,5

The relationship between parallax and distance in kilometers, light years and parsecs.
1 kilometer = .62 miles

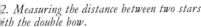

in German, and he also wrote popular books on astronomy for children in the primary grades. Everyday problems and scholarly theories were often intermingled in his work. One of his lesser works, for example, dealt with measuring the volume of truncated cones and conic sections. He started by talking about wine casks and how to fill them—an important task for the master of the house. The end product was a work that took its place in the history of mathematics as a precursor of integral calculus.

In Linz Kepler did some of his greatest and most challenging work. In his book, *De Harmonice Mundi,* he formulated his third law of planetary motion: it dealt with the mathematical relationship between the period of a planet (the time it took to complete its journey around the sun) and its distance from the sun. The book was completed in 1618, the same year that two Imperial officers were hurled out of a window in Prague, signaling the start of the Thirty Years' War.

This book picked up the thread of his first book on astronomy, *Mysterium Cosmographicum.* It attempted to provide a synthesis of all the sciences. On the basis of his Platonic geometry, he developed a cosmology, from which he then deduced laws governing music, geometry, astrology, politics, psychology, and everything else. In this attempt he came closer in spirit to the Pythagorean school and later mystics such as the Rosicrucians and the Cabbalists. But the important thing is that the work contained a basic law which inspired Newton to discover the law of gravity.

Kepler also wrote an *Epitome Astronomiae Copernicanae* (1621) and prepared the *Tabulae Rudolphinae* (1623). The *Epitome* actually presented Kepler's own system, and it was the most systematic treatment of astronomy since Ptolemy's *Almagest.* In it Kepler assigns the laws of planetary periodicity, gleaned from his observation of Mars, to the whole solar system; and for the first time we find a view of planetary motion that matches our view today. Kepler was far ahead of his contemporaries, because he had totally abandoned the epicycle theory. Galileo, on the other hand, still maintained the epicycle theory in his famous *Dialogue.*

The *Tabulae Rudolphinae* were planetary tables, and a most important contribution to practical astronomy. It was a stupendous piece of work, representing Kepler's collation of all Tycho Brahe's material. For more than a hundred years this work was to be the basic manual for all astronomers, calendar makers, and seafarers.

These two books cost Kepler much mental effort, and the course of outside events did not help the situation. The Thirty Years' War broke out in 1618. Danger and confusion reigned everywhere. In Linz, he was caught in political cross-currents. The expulsion of Protestants began, and once again the Jesuits came to Kepler's defense. In 1626 the rebellious Protestant peasants besieged the city, and Kepler's house was in the line of fire. His valuable books, manuscripts, and papers were in danger of being destroyed. When the siege was raised, Kepler decided to move to Ulm.

Kepler's last years were marked by increasing restlessness. Sick with fever and tormented with boils, he wandered from place to place. He often traveled on foot because he could not endure riding. Now a poor man, he had to borrow money on the way.

In Regensburg the Diet was in session. The Emperor owed him twelve thousand guilders. Kepler allowed his family to slip back into poverty without any hope of recovery. He arrived in Regensburg on an old mare, sold her for two guilders, and found a lodging for himself. Stricken with fever, he went to bed and never got up again. Lying silently on his bed, he would point to his head and then to the sky. He wished to make his peace, and ministers came to give him spiritual consolation. He died on November 15, 1630.

Kepler composed a Latin inscription for his own tombstone. His mind and spirit had been preoccupied with the heavens; now he sought rest for his body in the earth. But such was not to be. During the Thirty Years' War, his grave was desecrated and his remains were scattered.

43. Title page of the "Tabulae Rudolphinae" (1627). The center slab in the base depicts the island of Hven, where Brahe built his observatory. His measurements taken there were gathered together in these planetary tables. For the next century they served as the basis of all planetary calculations. The positions of the planets were accurately fixed within approximately a minute of arc.

THE ASTROPHYSICIST

During his last years, Kepler worked on his pet project, his book about an imaginary trip to the moon. It was finally published in 1634, four years after his death. Despite its rich vein of pure fantasy, the modernity of Kepler's outlook shone through clearly. He foreshadowed the modern scientific outlook in his conviction that the forces at work in the cosmos are physical in nature.

But Kepler did not make a complete break with the past. Though he regarded the sun as the prime mover of the planetary system, his conception was heavily tinged with mythical overtones. The sun stands at the center of the moving stars, itself at rest yet the source of motion; it is the image of God himself, the Father and Creator.

Kepler thought that his mystical geometry could unite theology and astronomy. Only at one point in his work do we find him breaking away from this outlook, but his remarks there presage the course which science would subsequently take. In the second edition of his *Astronomia Nova*, he remarked: "If we substitute the word 'force' for the word 'soul,' we shall have the basic principle which lies at the heart of my celestial physics. When I noticed that the force causing motion diminishes in power as the distance increases, just as sunlight diminishes in direct proportion to the distance from the sun, I came to the conclusion that this force had to be something material and substantial. And I use the word 'substantial' here as we use it in referring to light. By 'substantial' I mean some intangible quality emanating from a substantial corporeal body."

As the quotation from his letter shows (page 52), he had flashes of insight that were to light the way for later scientists. Kepler himself did not know about gravity and inertia. The laws of gravity and centrifugal force were not yet known; but Kepler surmised that physical forces were at work in the universe, and that they could be summed up in relatively simple formulae.

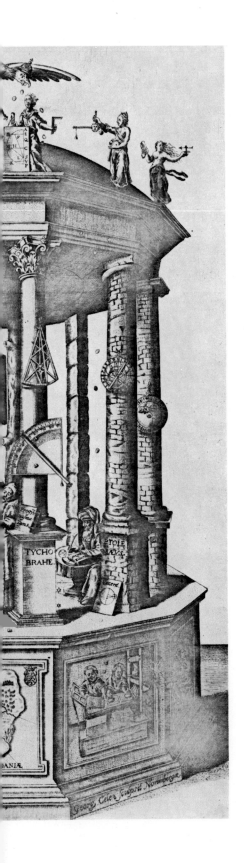

Kepler's three laws of planetary motion were to become the foundation of modern astrophysics. In his own works the laws were shrouded in mystical speculation and wild fantasies. He himself never united them in any systematic fashion. But there they were, and later astronomers and physicists adopted them to make further progress.

First Law

. . . Each planet moves around the sun along an ellipse, the sun being at one focus of the ellipse.

Second Law

. . . The radius vector of each planet (the line joining its center with that of the sun) moves over equal areas in equal times.

Third Law

. . . The square of the period of each planet's revolution around the sun is proportional to the cube of its mean distance from the sun.

Kepler's first and second law are found in his "Astronomia nova de motibus stellae Martis" (1609); his third law is found in "De Harmonice mundi" (1619)

GALILEO GALILEI

Born: February 15, 1564, in Pisa

Died: January 8, 1642, in Arcetri, near Florence

"IN MY CONFUSION AND UNCERTAINTY, MY MIND JUMPS FROM ONE OBJECT OF NATURE TO THE NEXT. I CANNOT PUT MY RESTLESS MIND AT EASE, NO MATTER HOW HARD I TRY. SLEEP HAS BECOME IMPOSSIBLE FOR ME IN THIS PREOCCUPIED STATE."

A letter of Galileo's, 1638

The previous page shows a portrait of Galileo from the Florence archives.

Right: View from the belfry of the Tower of Pisa. On the platform are two spheres, commemorating Galileo's demonstration of the laws governing falling bodies.

Left: In the tower of Pisa Galileo watched a new candelabrum swinging back and forth on a wire. He compared this oscillation with his own pulse, and thus discovered the usefulness of the pendulum in measuring time. He discovered that the pendulum's period of oscillation is independent of its amplitude. This discovery alone, made when Galileo was 19, would have merited him a place of honour in the history of physics.

Right: Galileo is supposed to have dropped wooden and lead balls from the tower of Pisa to prove his theory of falling bodies. Actually, the experiment was undertaken by those who opposed his theory. They hoped to prove him wrong. This is a view of the tower of Pisa from the palace of the Archbishop. On the table are two balls and a report on free fall by Galileo.

Galileo built many instruments himself. At the left is a pendulum clock. Shortly before his death Galileo invented a device combining a pendulum clockwork with a primitive watch escapement. The inventor of the modern pendulum clock was Huygens. In the foreground is a copy of Galileo's "Dialogue." In the background is a gallows with a magnet, holding a small Medici casket. To the right is Galileo's first telescope and his quadrant.

Left: In Florence Galileo worked under the protection of the Grand Duke of Tuscany, Cosimo II. Here he wrote his "Dialogue," which was dedicated to the Grand Duke. On the table are Galileo's instruments. Alongside the table is his astrolabe, now in the History of Science Museum in Florence.

Right: Galileo's rostrum in the old University of Padua. Enthusiastic students from all over Europe built the high platform for their short teacher, so that he could be seen from the back of the room. Many European noblemen, including the Crown Prince of Sweden, came to hear him lecture.

Next page: On the terrace of St. Mark's Cathedral in Venice, Galileo demonstrated his first telescope for the local senate.

THE MAN
BETWEEN TWO WORLDS

Kepler and Galileo were more closely united by their interest in the telescope than by their attitude towards the Copernican theory. Like Leonardo da Vinci, Kepler had hoped to get a better view of the stars with the aid of lenses before Galileo began to take optics seriously. But Galileo reacted more quickly when the first weak telescope was invented. Without any scientific knowledge of optics, Galileo soon improved the instrument.

The Dutch spectacle-grinder, Johann Lippershey, deserves to be called the inventor of the telescope. He was not granted a patent because several other people made a similar discovery at about the same time. The Frankfurt Fair was displaying telescopes of seven-power magnification, and in the spring of 1609 telescopes could be bought from opticians in Paris.

Galileo was a splendid mechanic and engineer. As soon as he heard about the new invention, he began to experiment with lenses. His first telescope had a magnifying power of 9. When others began to market telescopes of the same power, he started to build a more powerful instrument. With this instrument he discovered the moons of Jupiter, and his announcement of the discovery made him famous overnight.

In contrast to Kepler, who was given to mystical speculation and overawed by the vastness of the newly discovered universe, Galileo was a cool rationalist. He looked at the heavens with the eyes of a mechanic. His style of writing was not abstruse and baroque; it was straightforward, objective, and devoid of philosophical speculation. Perhaps that is the chief reason why Galileo soon came into conflict with the learned world of his day. His early conflicts were to pave the way for his later trial.

A BELLIGERENT SCIENTIST

Although the trial of Galileo came towards the end of his life, the seeds of conflict were sown much earlier. The underlying cause was the many heated quarrels which Galileo had with his opponents. The bitterness and acerbity of these disputes were due primarily to Galileo's temperament, not to the scientific questions at issue. Galileo was extremely rude and self-conceited. His first biographer, Viviani, tells us that even as a young student Galileo had heated arguments with his teachers and made them extremely angry. In his later arguments he added a dose of irony which did not help matters.

Galileo was extremely arrogant, and he loved to draw attention to himself. The

Left: The room where Galileo died at Arcetri near Florence. He spent his last years here under house arrest.

reserve of Kepler was totally alien to him. He only replied twice to Kepler's many letters, and he spurned the latter's suggestions of collaboration.

Galileo Galilei was born in Pisa on February 15, 1564. His father Vincenzo was a noted mathematician and a music lover, so Galileo grew up in an atmosphere of intellectual curiosity and cultural refinement. Whereas Kepler always retained spiritual and intellectual ties with the Middle Ages, Galileo was a modern man from the start. As a boy, he attended the Jesuit school of Vallombroso near Florence; later he went to the University of Pisa. At eighteen he was already regarded as having overbearing character.

Galileo argued with his teachers over the Aristotelian view of the universe. He invented physical devices and discovered physical data. Although he was supposed to study medicine, he spent more time on applied mechanics. It was thus that he discovered how to measure the pulse of sick patients. Failing to receive a university grant, he continued to study privately. He soon made friends with the nobility, and eventually became a protégé of Ferdinand de Medici, the ruler of Florence.

With the backing of this prince, he became a lecturer in mathematics at the University of Pisa when he was twenty-five. At twenty-eight he was made a full professor of mathematics in the University of Padua. In his official capacity he taught the Ptolemaic system, and did not promulgate the Copernican view. He did not publish any printed works; all we have are his lectures and some handwritten papers.

His fame during this period rested on his mechanical inventions. For decades he did not publish anything at Pisa about his investigations into the laws of falling bodies or of pendular motion. It is almost as if he wanted to protect his discoveries from misunderstanding and premature publication. At this point one might have taken him for another Copernicus.

But the air of peace did not last. After several years of quiet research, Galileo got into his first big argument. He wrote an insignificant paper describing an improvement he had made in some device. A year later a mathematician, Balthasar Capra, wrote a paper on the same subject, borrowing a few ideas from Galileo; but he had the temerity to criticize him on several points. In 1607 Galileo published a pamphlet bristling with insults and abusive language. In it he also attacked his opponent's teacher, the astronomer Simon Marius, who later discovered the Andromeda nebula. The virulent pamphlet was eventually confiscated, and thus ended round one of Galileo's running battle with other scholars.

The next round brought Galileo before the city council of Venice. He gave the city his first telescope; in return, his income was doubled and he was granted a professorship for life. Soon afterwards, one could buy an equally powerful telescope at any optician's shop for a small sum. The reaction of the city populace was immediate and vehement.

44. In 1610 Galileo observed the moon through a telescope for the first time. He saw the ragged border between light and shadow, and concluded that it had a mountainous surface. This conclusion was verified by the observation of mountains standing clearly in the light. From the length of certain shadows, Galileo calculated the height of the moon's mountains.

45. Galileo published his findings on the phases of Venus, proving Copernicus was right in saying that they must be like the phases of the moon.

His next big quarrel was with the Jesuits. It developed into a bitter controversy with a Jesuit scholar, and foreshadowed his later conflicts with the Order. It is not surprising that Galileo should come into conflict with the conservative scholars of the Aristotelian school. But only his bitter personal attacks on Jesuit scholars can explain their eventual hostility towards him. The Jesuits favored scientific progress, and they were not at all antagonistic to Galileo at the start.

Shortly after the publication in 1610 of *Sidereus Nuncius (The Celestial Messenger)*, Galileo tried to show the moons of Jupiter to a group of conservative professors. None of them could see the moons when they looked through his telescope. The instrument was hard to use, and some even refused to look through it. The chief opponent of Galileo's view was Magini, the astronomy professor at Bologna. His assistant wrote a pamphlet which rejected the findings of Galileo's book.

Galileo's reaction was typical. He cited the support of Kepler, even though he ignored Kepler's contributions and never thanked him for them. Upon the death of the philosopher Libri, another opponent of his views, Galileo remarked sarcastically that Libri "may now see in heaven what he refused to see on earth."

At this point, however, one of Galileo's chief opponents reversed his position. Clavius, the best known Jesuit mathematician and astronomer, began to observe the stars along with his colleagues. They scrutinized Saturn and the phases of Venus. They made precise calculations and reported their findings to the Order and to high officials in the Church. As a result, Galileo was received in audience by Pope Paul V in 1611, and given high praise.

Throughout Europe, other Jesuit astronomers began to occupy themselves with the new discoveries and to revise the older views. They studied comets, the "earthly nature" of the moon, and sunspots. The renowned Jesuit astronomer from Ingolstadt, Christoph Scheiner, had discovered sunspots and had observed them for a long time. In 1612 his work on sunspots was published, and he sent copies to Kepler and Galileo to get their views. Kepler replied promptly. Galileo sent a reply three months later, claiming that he had discovered the sunspots long ago. He could not admit that other scientists might discover something new in the heavens.

With regard to the physical nature of sunspots, Galileo was right and Scheiner wrong. The latter regarded them as passing bodies, whereas Galileo said they were part of the sun's surface. He felt that sunspots proved that the sun, too, turns on its axis, thus openly acknowledging the Copernican view for the first time. But his senseless debate over who had discovered them first, lost him the sympathy of Jesuit scholars.

The next round began when Galileo ventured into the field of theology in the course of his debates. Various professors had looked to the Bible for support when they attempted to refute Galileo's theories. None of these professors was a theologian, however, and Galileo actually had the support of many theologians. But now Galileo himself began to argue theologically. He wanted to force theologians to openly support the Copernican view instead of merely tolerating it. If they could not prove the opposite view, then they should give theological support to Copernicus! Galileo had gone beyond the boundaries of science and stepped into the sanctuary.

On the fourth Sunday of Advent in 1614, the Dominican preacher Caccini openly attacked Galileo's views in Florence. He called mathematics an invention of the devil and accused Galileo of atheism. To support his views, he cited the book of Joshua which talks about the sun and moon standing still at God's command.

The attack was the view of one man, not of his Order. Other Dominicans defended Galileo, but now the scholarly debate had become a public affair. Turmoil ensued, and letters went back and forth between Church officials. Soon an inquiry began in Rome, based on a letter which Galileo had written a year earlier to the Grand Duchess Christina. In this letter Galileo had come out in favour of the Copernican theory without presenting any proof for it. Now, a year later, Galileo said that his opponents view must prove their case. Instead of proving his case, he had shifted the burden of proof onto the Church. Galileo's letter came out in several versions, and the copy which reached Rome would seem to have been altered. The Holy Office had no alternative but to make an investigation.

In 1615 Galileo made his second trip to Rome. It was not a triumphant visit, and his first "trial" took place. It was alleged that Galileo was summoned to Rome by the Inquisition, but that is not true. He made the trip on his own, against the advice of Archduke Cosimo. But Galileo still had influential friends in Rome. The Jesuit Clavius, the leading astronomer in Rome, stood by him; other Jesuit scholars took up his observations and carried them further. His friend and patron, Cardinal Barberini, who later became Pope Urban VIII, offered him his protection. And many in the Vatican lent him their support.

Galileo's chief adversary was Cardinal Bellarmine. Sixteen years earlier, Bellarmine had been a member of the Inquisition which tried Giordano Bruno. But the seventy-three-year-old Bellarmine was no grand inquisitor. He was a cultured, educated man who led an ascetic life. One of his own books was later put on the Index for a time, and still later he was canonized a saint. He was so highly regarded as a theologian that his opinion was valued more than that of Pope Paul V.

Bellarmine was wise enough to propose a compromise in the letter which he sent to Galileo through a third party. He suggested indirectly that one might be permitted to propose the Copernican theory as a hypothesis, and to maintain that it was superior to the Ptolemaic hypothesis. But he made it clear that it was up to the proponents of the Copernican theory to prove their case.

The exchange of letters was handled by Cardinal Dini. Once again Galileo was

46. *A Jesuit priest, Christoph Scheiner discovered sunspots independently of Galileo (Ingolstadt, March 1611). Scheiner sits at a table while another priest verifies his observations. The sunlight strikes the telescope from the left. The sun is projected on a piece of paper placed in the casing. Scheiner's*

arrogant and virulent. He called Bellarmine a "peripatetic Aristotelian, who would be incapable of following the simplest and most obvious line of proof." Moreover, he suggested that the Church's tolerance of the Copernican theory up to then was conclusive proof of its accuracy.

That is how matters stood when Galileo arrived in Rome in early December 1615. Caccini and other witnesses were already there to testify against him; but the Inquisition put little faith in what they had to say. Caccini was already regarded as a fanatic, and the countless contradictions in his testimony convinced no one. The case was dropped because of the inauthenticities in Galileo's alleged letter.

Galileo was uncommonly active during his stay in Rome. He discussed his theories and debated opposing views at every opportunity. A contemporary, Monsignor Querengo, described his tactics with relish: "The best part of it was that he took his opponents' point of view first, and made a better case for their position than they could have. Then he would demolish it with his own arguments, making them look all the more ridiculous."

So Galileo argued and intrigued for his own position and prestige. While he was preparing to send the Pope a new theory on tides — to support the heliocentric view of the universe and to prove the earth's rotation — the Holy Office was convoked on February 19, 1616. Four days later it came out against the Copernican theory: it was heretical and contradicted the teaching of Scripture. But thanks to the efforts of several scholarly Cardinals, the original text of this decision was not published for seventeen years; and the word "heresy" was struck from the text before publication. Moreover, Galileo's name did not appear in the document, nor were his books put on the Index. Only Copernicus's work was put on the Index, and in its original version it remained there for only four years. In 1620 an emended version appeared, in which his nine theses on the heliocentric theory were altered or dropped.

No public attempt was made to humiliate Galileo. Cardinal Bellarmine was commissioned by the Pope to admonish him privately. There are conflicting views as to what actually happened. Some say that Galileo was forbidden to discuss the Copernican theory. But this is challenged by the fact that Cardinal Bellarmine issued a certificate, attesting that Galileo had not foresworn his teaching and that he had not been given any penance. He had merely been informed of the contents of the decree. In any case, Galileo was received in audience by the Pope.

With Cardinal Bellarmine's letter of safe conduct in his pocket, Galileo returned to Florence. For the next eight years he lived as a famous man, and worked away unmolested. In 1618 he was supposed to have made his last observations and calculations on the moons of Jupiter.

That same year he became involved in another dispute with a Jesuit. Three comets appeared in the heavens, almost as if they were harbingers of the Thirty Years' War. Father Grassi, a Jesuit, delivered a lecture on them and challenged the traditional Aristotelian view. He assigned regular orbits to them, similar to those of the planets, and asserted that part of their orbit was farther from the earth than the moon. Galileo had one of his students write an offensive retort to this view, maintaining that comets were of earthly origin. Father Grassi wrote another paper in response. Once again

assistant can easily see the sunspots. On the table lies a report of his observations. Basically the same principle is used to observe sunspots today.
The illustration is from the frontispiece of Scheiner's book, "Rosa ursina."

Galileo prepared to reply. But this time he was more circumspect. He spent two years on his article "The Assayer," and he avoided insulting remarks. His work passed the censor in Rome and appeared in 1623, just when his friend and patron, Cardinal Barberini, was enthroned as Pope Urban VIII.

It was a time of triumph for Galileo. He had made new enemies among the Jesuits, but his friend was now Pope. Urban VIII invited him to Rome. The sixty-year-old Galileo, not in the best of health, hastened to accept the invitation and set out on his third trip to Rome.

He received a hero's welcome. He was greeted everywhere as a great thinker. Despite his own political problems, Pope Urban VIII had six long meetings with him. The Pope spoke frankly about his objections to the Copernican theory, but he said nothing about revoking the decree of 1616. Galileo, however, was now convinced that he could carry on his own work as he saw fit. Laden with gifts, he returned to Florence.

THE IMPRUDENT DIALOGUE

For a year, Galileo labored over his magnum opus. Already a widower, he was cared for by his daughter Virginia. In this period scholarly criticism of him abated, and he was accorded respect by many learned men. It was in this atmosphere of respect that he wrote his *Dialogue On The Two Systems Of The World*.

The *Dialogue* is a discussion between three people that lasts for four days. One person represents the Aristotelian view of the universe; one represents the Copernican view (as seen by Galileo); and another is an uncommitted but intelligent bystander. The Aristotelian spokesman, Simplicio, is made to look ridiculous by the Copernican spokesman, Salviati, and the intelligent bystander, Sagredo. But Galileo was imprudent. He had Simplicio reiterate the favorite argument of Pope Urban VIII against the Copernican theory. His friend the Pope eventually took revenge on Galileo for this indiscretion.

When the manuscript was finished, Galileo made his fourth trip to Rome (1630). Again he was received cordially by the Pope. He asked the Pope to give the book his *Imprimatur*. Urban VIII, entangled in political problems of his own, sidestepped the matter and entrusted it to the Roman censor, Father Riccardi. The latter agreed to give his permission, provided that the President of the *Accademia dei Lincei* approved, and that it was printed in Rome. Galileo returned to Florence, rejected these conditions, and made two demands: 1) the book must be printed in Florence; 2) someone in Florence, not Riccardi, should censor it. Galileo finally persuaded Riccardi to accept a censor who was totally loyal to himself.

The first copies rolled off the presses in February 1632, and reaction was not long in coming. Galileo's enemies hastened to show the Pope what Galileo had done to him in the book. The Pope felt that he had been betrayed and ridiculed by his friend.

47. *Various ways of using optical devices. On the left, a typical telescope. On the right, a special telescope for observing the sun. Left foreground, two different methods of solar observation: 1) by projection on a bright surface; 2) by optical alignment with a reflecting mirror.*
Frontispiece for Book 3 of "Rosa ursina."

Rome sent orders to the printer in Florence, telling him to halt the sale of the book. On October 1, 1632, Galileo was ordered to appear before the Inquisition. He managed to gain a postponement by getting three doctors to testify to his ill-health. But on January 20, 1633, he had to set out for Rome. His fifth trip to Rome took place during the winter, and he was transported on a stretcher.

The first hearing took place on April 12. He was charged with disobeying the command not to discuss the Copernican theory. Galileo appealed to Cardinal Bellarmine's letter, where no such command appeared. He also tried to get the case dismissed, claiming that he had proved the very opposite of the Copernican theory. Fortunately for him, the Inquisitors did not pursue that point and reveal his lie.

At the second hearing, scholarly experts gave their testimony. They forced Galileo to renounce his claim that his *Dialogue* was written to disprove the Copernican theory. This time he maintained that he had fallen into error, but that no evil intent was involved. He had merely delighted in his own ability to formulate false proofs. If he were given another chance, he would willingly reformulate these proofs, so that no one would be convinced by them.

The third hearing was a mere formality. Galilei read a paper in his defense. In it he appealed to his "wretched physical condition" and to his age. He also stated that he had no longer any doubts about the truth of the Ptolemaic view.

Galileo never spoke the famous words attributed to him: *"Eppur si muove"* ("And yet it does move"). He simply recanted, and that is all the Inquisition wanted. They merely wished to reprimand him, not to destroy him. Therefore they did not pursue the truth or falsehood of his statements.

Galileo had to wait six weeks for the final verdict. His book was condemned. Galileo himself was to renounce his views under threat of torture, and then be sent to prison. These punishments were soon set aside, and he was put under house arrest. His daughter, who had become a Carmelite nun, was to read the prescribed penitential psalms for him. The hardest punishment was the renunciation of his own convictions. He was even ordered to denounce to the Inquisition all his students and friends who held the Copernican view.

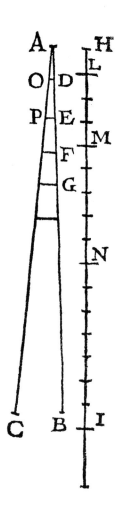

48. *Galileo depicted his theory of falling bodies with these diagrams. The diagram on the upper left was used to determine the rate of motion of a falling body. The scale on the right depicts the distance covered at a uniform rate of acceleration. The diagram below depicts the combination of a uniform (not accelerated) horizontal motion and an accelerated vertical motion; the resulting curve is a parabola (only one leg shown).*
By many experiments Galileo established two points: 1) all free-falling bodies have an even rate of acceleration; 2) a thrown projectile maintains its horizontal component, taking the path of a parabola.

THE SECOND DIALOGUE

But that was not the last to be heard from Galileo Galilei. Many great men came to visit him at his home. Four years before his death he was visited by John Milton, the author of *Paradise Lost*. In 1636 he was visited by his former pupil, Count Noailles, who was now the French Papal Nuncio; and Galileo presented him with a new manuscript entitled *Dialogue On The Two New Sciences*. Again his three characters are involved in a discussion, examining all the problems of physics on which Galileo had spent his life. The manuscript was smuggled out of the country and published in Leyden, Holland. The next year Galileo went blind.

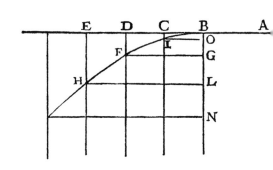

GALILEO: THE TELESCOPE AND ASTRONOMY

Galileo's contribution to the scientific exploration of space is assessed very differently by various people. Two hundred years after his death, the French mathematician Lagrange asserted that his work in physics was incomparably greater than his work in astronomy. The former showed real genius; the latter merely involved pointing a telescope towards the heavens.

HIS ASTRONOMICAL DISCOVERIES

However, Galileo's work in astronomy did provide major proofs for the validity of the Copernican system (see page 37; picture p. 15). In observing Venus, and later Mars, he saw the phases which had to exist according to Copernicus. On January 7, 1610, Galileo saw the four moons of Jupiter. It was probably his most important astronomical observation because it proved conclusively that there was *more than one* center of motion in the universe. It further proved that a center of motion could also be in motion itself. Both these notions were unthinkable in the classical view. His observations of sunspots also challenged the Aristotelian view, because he concluded that they were of solar origin and that the sun probably rotated on its own axis. Galileo used the magnifying power of the telescope; and in his observations of the fixed stars and the Milky Way, he discovered the light-gathering power of the telescope. Looking through the eyepiece, he at once saw countless stars that no human eye had ever seen before. The Milky Way showed up as a conglomeration of "telescopic" stars. These astronomical observations prove that Galileo was a keen-eyed observer; and his study of free-fall proves that he was a masterly experimenter. His theory of free-fall was undoubtedly his greatest innovation, for it represented a complete break with traditional teaching. He had some vague notions about the force of gravity, which caused the stone to fall to the ground according to fixed laws; but it was Newton who established a connection between this force and the force that kept the planets in orbit.

THE USES OF THE TELESCOPE

Galileo's telescope was a patchwork affair, even though Kepler provided the theory for a lens telescope in his book on dioptrics (1611). For this work alone Kepler deserves a place of honor in the history of astronomy.

The chief purpose of the telescope is to enlarge the viewing angle, so that distant

Galileo's record of the various positions of Jupiter's 4 moons on successive days.

objects seem to be brought up close. This magnification is very important when we are dealing with objects such as the moon, the sun, or the planets. In connection with the stars and other more distant objects, the light-gathering capacity of the telescope is much more important. The large object lens (objective) can take in much more light than the pupil of the human eye.

This quality becomes even more obvious when we use a photographic plate as the light-receiver. The photographic film is designed to accumulate the light that falls on it. A weak light source, no longer perceptible to the human eye, becomes visible on a photographic film so long as it is exposed long enough. Herein lies the reason for astronomy's progress in the study of distant and fainter galaxies.

LIGHT RAYS: DIRECTION AND BRIGHTNESS

We can study various qualities of incoming starlight: its direction, its quantity, and its quality. To ask about its direction is equivalent to asking the location of the star in the heavens. Even in ancient times coordinate grids had been worked out to pinpoint the location of a star, just as we would determine the length and width of a place on earth. But today we usually start out by using a meridian circle to observe the basic star in the given system; then, using photographic plates for further observations, we make additional measurements in terms of the basic star already plotted.

Photography helps us in two basic ways. Firstly, the longer exposure time enables us to glimpse fainter stars than we could see with our eyes alone. Secondly, the photographic plate is a valuable document in our observations. Time, in a certain sense, is the one big variable in celestial observation; and the photographic plate gives us a picture of the heavens at the precise moment of observation. Two pictures, taken sufficiently far apart in time (e.g. 50 years), will show that many of the "fixed" stars have shifted their position slightly. This is their own distinctive pattern of motion, not an illusory pattern caused by the earth's motion.

Clearly then, when the direction from which the starlight comes is a factor, the astronomer exploits the capacity of the telescope to enlarge the viewing angle. The greater the focal length, the larger the viewing angle.

When the researcher chooses to use a telescope with a large aperture, he is probably interested in the quantity of light involved—that is, the brightness of the object. Here the light-gathering capacity of the telescope plays a major role.

With the naked eye we can see about 6,000 stars. In antiquity these stars were divided into six major classes representing divine hierarchies. The basic criterion was the chronological order in which they became visible in the evening sky. The brightest stars, the ones seen first, were put in magnitude 1; the next brightest were put in magnitude 2, and so on down the line.

As this empirical scale was being reworked more scientifically, people discovered that there were even brighter stars around than those of magnitude 1. With the telescope they could also see fainter stars than those of magnitude 6. As a result, the

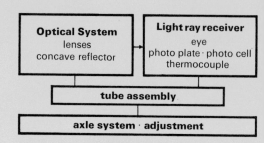

Structure of an astronomical telescope

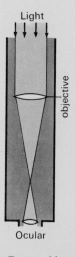

Course of beam in a refractor telescope

Absorption in the earth's atmosphere at various altitudes above sea level and at different wave lengths. The optimal working zone for balloons, rockets, and satellites is indicated. 1 km = .62 miles.

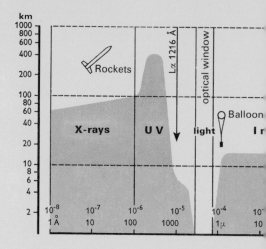

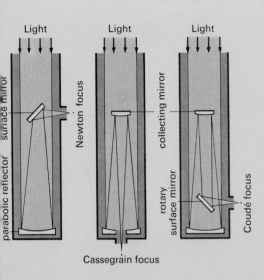

Light   Light   Light

parabolic reflector surface mirror

Newton focus

collecting mirror

rotary surface mirror

Coudé focus

Cassegrain focus

Course of beam in a reflector telescope: three designs

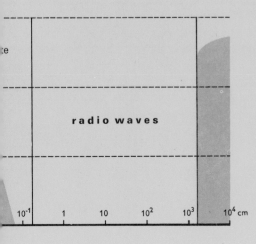

radio waves

10^{-1} 1 10 10^2 10^3 10^4 cm

basic scale had to be broadened at both ends, to incorporate negative values for extreme brightness and higher numbers for extreme faintness. Sirius, the brightest star in the heavens, was given a magnitude of —1.5. A star so faint that it can only be seen with a 100 inch telescope would have a magnitude of +19.

As soon as men began to correlate the brightness of the stars with their distance from earth, they naturally discovered that the stars do not shine with equal brightness. Their *luminosity* was now studied as an individual characteristic. It was discovered, for example, that the star Vega in the constellation of Lyra has an illuminating power 60 times that of our own sun; and the luminosity of the star Rigel in the constellation of Orion is 21,000 times that of our own sun.

Now we have other ways of determining the luminosity of a star (e.g. through the use of the spectrum), and this is important. If we know the luminosity of a star and then consider its apparent brightness, we have a chance to judge its distance. If two stars have equal illuminating power but different distances from earth, the more distant star will appear fainter. This difference in brightness can be measured, and then converted into a measurement of distance.

The brightness of a star can be measured directly with the aid of photometers. It can also be calculated indirectly by taking photographs of the heavens and examining the individual star images.

THE OPTICAL WINDOW

Lens telescopes gave rise to certain optical flaws (e.g. color aberration). As a result, people began to look for other optical devices that would not have these flaws. Newton found his answer in reflecting telescopes (reflectors); it produced an image through *reflection,* and made use of eyepiece lenses. The lens telescopes (refractors), by contrast, produced the picture through *refraction*. Both basic types are used in astronomy, and there are many variations on each. But because there are many practical difficulties in building giant refractors, most large instruments are reflectors.

In the last thirty years the technique of astronomical observation has made enormous progress. Astronomy has greatly improved its instruments. Even more important is the fact that its range of observation has been greatly extended, and we must understand how this has come about.

Visible light is an electromagnetic wave emission with wave lengths between 3,900 and 7,000 angstrom units (1 angstrom unit = 0.000 0001 mm.). Shorter wave lengths (ultraviolet) cannot be observed on the earth's surface because they are absorbed in the ozone layer of the atmosphere. Longer wave lengths (infrared) cannot be seen because they are absorbed by the water vapor and carbon dioxide in the earth's atmosphere. For this reason we talk about an "optical window" in the atmosphere, which allows only certain wave lengths to be seen.

But the atmosphere has other effects on astronomical observation as well. It is not homogeneous in its makeup. There are layers of air with different temperatures and different densities. Their intercontact in the atmosphere produces turbulence which blurs the image we get in the telescope. The theoretical capabilities of the telescope are never fully realized in actual practice. Moreover, the light coming from the stars interacts with the atoms and molecules in our atmosphere. As a result, light is scattered and our atmosphere has its own peculiar lighting effect. That is why the daylight sky is blue, and why we cannot see the stars in the daytime.

RADIO ASTRONOMY

The earth's atmosphere opens up once again for wave lengths ranging between several millimeters and 15 meters. This is the realm of radio waves, so we talk about a "radio window" in the atmosphere. Waves under one millimeter are absorbed by water vapor in the atmosphere; waves over about 15 meters will not penetrate the ionosphere.

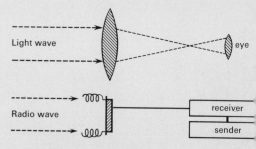

The light telescope (top) and the radio telescope (bottom) are similarly constructed.

To the average person, size is the most obvious and striking difference between the optical telescope and the radio telescope. The radio telescope is enormous, yet it has a basic flaw: its resolving power, that is, its power to distinguish between two closely associated objects, is very poor. This flaw can be reduced by building the radio telescope as a giant parabolic reflector (over 300 feet in diameter!), or as an interferometer complex with a base length of several miles.

The radio window was discovered by an American, Karl Jansky, in 1932. While seeking the source of radio interference, he discovered that radio signals were constantly coming from outside the solar system. Radio astronomy began to develop on a large scale towards the end of World War II, when it was discovered that the sun was apparently the source of interference to certain army radar devices.

The giant radio telescope which it was proposed to build at Sugar Grove in West Virginia. Overall height: over 600 feet. Reflector diameter: over 500 feet. Weight: 20,000 tons. The construction was abandoned.

EXTRA-TERRESTRIAL ASTRONOMY

Through the use of high altitude balloons and rockets in the last two decades, we have begun to circumvent the influence of the earth's atmosphere. Astronomical observation is now probing into the shortest waves of the electromagnetic spectrum: ultraviolet waves from the sun, X-rays from various stellar bodies, and gamma quanta. We now have much more information about cosmic radiation, not to mention our newly developed research into particle radiation.

Besides this, we have already managed to use special space capsules for moon landings and overflights of other planets. These vehicles have conducted special studies far outside the influence of the earth's atmosphere. Astronomy thus has reached a point where it can study the heavenly bodies more directly than it could before. Newton was ingenious enough to ask himself an important question: Was the force that caused a body to fall to earth the same force that kept the moon in orbit around the earth, the planets in orbit around the sun, and the moons of Jupiter around that planet?

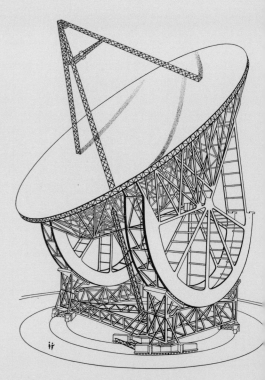

12*

9. Frontispiece of Galileo's "Dialogue On the World System."

Galileo Galilei died on January 8, 1642, at the age of seventy-eight. The chief Inquisitor of Florence brought a papal blessing to him, but he was denied burial in the family plot. No funeral mass was held, and no memorial was erected. He was laid to rest in an unmarked tomb in a small side-chapel of Santa Croce.

A WORLD IN CRISIS

Although Galileo opposed the Aristotelian world-picture throughout his life, he never fully demolished it. He never managed to prove conclusively the truth of the Copernican theory or to make it absolutely victorious. Up to his day mathematics had concerned itself mainly with quantitative dimensions of length, area, and volume. Galileo applied mathematics to other measurable realities. He began to measure the quantitative relationships between time, motion, and matter. Thus he contributed a modern, mechanistic line of argument in favor of the Copernican theory. On the whole, Galileo did more to popularize the Copernican theory than did Kepler. But this was due more to his use of the telescope than to his mechanistic arguments. The moons of Jupiter, the phases of Venus, and the mountains on the moon were more convincing arguments than Kepler's laws of planetary motion. Perhaps that is why Galileo provoked a reaction against the Copernican view and a setback to the progress of astronomy.

Galileo's popularization of the Copernican view seemed to be in direct conflict with the teachings of faith and seemed to offer a threat to Christian belief. Moreover, Galileo had managed to antagonize forward-looking Jesuits, as well as the Pope and conservative scholars. But perhaps the real roots of the conflict lay in the intellectual outlook of the day. The human mind had undergone a renaissance, but the life of faith had not been similarly revitalized. Man's soul was in crisis between two worlds.

Perhaps this existential crisis is best exemplified by the life of the French scientist, Blaise Pascal, whom we shall consider next.

BLAISE PASCAL

Born: June 19, 1623, in Clermont   Died: August 19, 1662, in Paris

"HERE WAS A MAN WHO HAD ALREADY ENCOMPASSED THE WHOLE EXPANSE OF HUMAN KNOWLEDGE, IN AN AGE WHEN MOST MEN WERE SCARCELY AWARE OF ITS DIMENSIONS. THEN, RECOGNIZING THE VANITY OF IT ALL, HE TURNED WHOLLY TO RELIGION."

Chateaubriand on Blaise Pascal

The previous page shows a portrait of Blaise Pascal from the Louvre in Paris.

Right: At the monastery of Port Royal des Champs, Pascal studied Jansen's commentaries on the works of St. Augustine. By the window of his cell are Pascal's Jansenist Bible and crucifix, an hour-glass, and pages of his manuscripts.

The Les Granges estate dominates
the valley of Port Royal des
Champs. Here the inhabitants of
the Port Royal monastery spent
their time in meditation. But a
water supply had to be obtained.
Pascal solved the problem with a
power-driven winch. He himself
often drew water with a
wooden bucket.

Left: At eighteen Pascal invented a calculating machine to help his father. He then successfully marketed it himself. Some of these "Pascalines" are still in existence.

Right: At Puy-de-Dôme the twenty-five-year-old Pascal used a mercury tube to investigate the decrease in air pressure in relation to height as one ascends a mountain.

Next page: In ill-health Pascal retired to the monastery of Port Royal des Champs near Paris. Here he took walks, discussing metaphysical questions with his friends.

+

L'an de grâce 1654

Lundy 23 novembre jour de S' Clement pape et martir et autres
au martyrologe.
Veille de S' Chrisogone martir et autres,
Depuis environ dix heures et demy du soir jusques environ minuit et demy,

FEU.

Dieu d'Abraham, Dieu d'Isaac, Dieu de Jacob.
non des philosophes et des savants.
Certitude. Certitude. Sentiment. Joie. Paix.
Dieu de Jesus Christ.

A SCIENTIST REJECTS SCIENCE

Ten years after Galileo's death, a scientific genius named Blaise Pascal underwent a spiritual experience. It was not a medieval vision peopled with angels and devils. It was a night of religious fire that seared the very marrow of his soul, and a radical conversion which affected his whole future life. We catch a glimpse of the experience in the powerful lines he wrote to commemorate it; he carried a parchment copy of the manuscript sewn to the lining of his coat, and called it the *Memorial*:

FIRE

God of Abraham, Isaac, and Jacob,
Not of philosophers and scholars.
Certainty, Certainty, Emotion! Joy! Peace!
God of Jesus Christ.
Deum meum et deum vestrum.
"Thy God shall be my God."
Oblivion of the world and of everything, except God.
He can only be found by the ways taught by the Gospel.

Ah, the wonder of the human soul.
"Righteous Father, the world has not known thee,
but I have known thee."
Joy! Joy! Joy! Tears of Joy!
I have separated myself from him.
Dereliquerunt me fontes aquae vivae.
"My God, why has thou forsaken me?"
Let me not be separated from him eternally!
This is eternal life, that they should know that
thou art the only true God, and him whom
thou hast sent: Jesus Christ.

Jesus Christ, Jesus Christ.
I have cut myself off from him.
I fled him.
I denied him and crucified him.
Let me never be separated from him!
He can only be kept by the ways taught in the Gospel.
Total and delicious renunciation!

Left: Pascal's testament, crucifix and penitential chain.

The man who wrote these words was one of the outstanding scientists of his day. A shrewd businessman who had successfully carried through several marketing ventures, he also invented the first truly functional calculating machine. In his younger days he had been something of a dandy. He assumed courtly airs, his sister reports, "as if he had breathed that atmosphere all his life." In dealing with other people he was arrogant and conceited. His air of intellectual superiority made him appear something of a snob. Then, suddenly, he grew disgusted with the world of men and withdrew into himself. Three months later, the great conversion took place.

A few days after his experience, Pascal added another comment to his diary: "Complete self-abandonment to Jesus Christ and my spiritual director. Eternal happiness for a day of suffering on earth. *Non obliviscar sermones tuos.* Amen." Suddenly this wordly man, as proud and as arrogant as Galileo had been, began to talk of "complete self-abandonment." Was Pascal renouncing science, was he rejecting empirical research and mathematical calculation? Had he given up the effort to understand the world by quantitative methods? In effect, the answer is "yes."

THE GREAT RENUNCIATION

Pascal was not an astronomer, but he was one of the leading scientists and mathematicians of his day. He was familiar with the theories of Copernicus and Galileo; but he was overawed by the vastness of the universe which they had opened up. He saw it as a huge, empty void that could only strike terror into man's heart. Kepler, too, had been somewhat overawed by the new conception of the universe that he had helped to formulate; but he kept at his work. He had not found any contradiction between his faith and his scientific research. Pascal, on the other hand, did see a contradiction between the two. He examined the problem and tried to resolve this contradiction. As a result, he chose the course that was forced upon Galileo by others.

Galileo was forced to deny his scientific convictions. Pascal renounced his of his own free will. Reactions to Pascal's choice have been varied. Some have found his action praiseworthy, such as Chateaubriand, for whom Pascal had abandoned the entire range of human scientific knowledge, exchanging its futility for religion. Paul Valéry, however, was not so favorably impressed by Pascal's decision. "He chose to misuse the most important talents he had been given, his powers of analysis and his wholly admirable genius for expression, thus falsifying what before was clear and far from lamentable ... I am instinctively reminded of the intolerable noise a dog makes when baying at the moon." Romano Guardini summed up the paradox in a single sentence: "He let the problems stand, and placed his heart in God's hands."

50. On September 19, 1648, Pascal lets his brother-in-law test air pressure on Puy-de-Dôme. It decreases as the altitude increases. This is one of the most important experiments in the history of science. The sea of air in which we live is subject to changes conditioned by both time and place. One of the basic principles of meteorology was thus discovered.

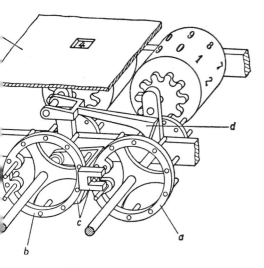

) unit gear, b) tens gear, c) tens gearshift,
) trip dog, e) cover plate with sight aperture.

1. Diagrammatic picture of Pascal's
alculating machine. Pascal decided to
ombine several gear wheels, associating
ach gear with a place in the decimal system
i.e. units, tens, hundreds, etc.). The special
eature of the machine was the use of a
en-carrier, which switched to the next
ighest number when passing from
* to 0.

Was Pascal a great religious figure, like Augustine or Kierkegaard? Or was he a philosopher, driven into the arms of religion by the human condition? These questions are not easy to answer. Perhaps it is best to follow the stages in his career as clearly as we can.

Blaise Pascal was born in Clermont-Ferrand on June 19, 1623. He was a sickly child, bedeviled by fits of weakness which some imputed to a witch's curse. He had two sisters, Gilberte, who was three years older, and Jacqueline, who was a year younger than himself. His mother died soon after the birth of his younger sister. Blaise's father, Étienne, was a distinguished civil servant who soon brought his children to Paris, where he moved in learned circles. He even became involved in debates with Descartes.

The widower was a zealous teacher of his children, whose education he undertook himself. At the age of twelve, his young son Blaise reformulated Euclid's first thirty-two theorems; at twelve, together with some friends, his youngest daughter Jacqueline wrote a full-length comedy in verse which they performed before a large audience. When their father rebelled against a tax decree and was threatened with imprisonment, after playing Cassandra in a children's performance at the Hôtel de Richelieu, Jacqueline made an appeal in verse to the Cardinal, and won her father a pardon.

The father did not hesitate to encourage the talents of his young geniuses. He often brought them with him to learned meetings in academic circles. At sixteen, Blaise wrote a commentary on conic sections. In her biography of her brother, Gilberte reports that "it was the most masterly piece of work since the days of Archimedes." The whole tone of her biography indicates that Gilberte idolized her younger brother and was very much a substitute-mother for him.

The whole family atmosphere fostered young Blaise's interest in learning and scholarship. When Blaise made his own discovery of Euclid's theorems at sixteen, his father was astounded. Gilberte described what happened: "My father was speechless at the extent of his talent, and he went to show his work to a friend and fellow scholar, Monsieur Le Pailleur. The latter could not imagine why my father was in such a state, weeping and wringing his hands. He asked him why he was so sad. My father replied: 'I'm weeping for joy. You know how I have tried to distract him from geometry, for fear that his other studies would suffer. But look what he has come up with.' My father then showed him my brother's work. It was almost as if he had invented mathematics."

The forceful figure of his father, personally self-effacing yet ever anxious to further the progress of his son, probably sowed the seeds of conflict in Blaise's own heart. His father had taught him that the authority of science must never be confused with the authority of faith. The articles of faith could never be made subject to the rule of reason. In his essay on Pascal, Reinhold Schneider has written, "The distinction made by his father may well have paved the way for his own final option."

But that choice was still in the future. At nineteen, Pascal produced his most famous and astounding invention: the calculating machine. The first mechanical of the computer, it was invented (in 1642, the year Galileo died) in order to simplify the tax work he did for his father. Three years later he presented the finished machine to the French Chancellor. A patent was made out in favor of Blaise Pascal in 1649, and his definitive version of the machine was completed in 1652.

In 1648, together with his father, Blaise followed up some earlier investigations into the existence of the vacuum. For these experiments they used the new barometer invented by Torricelli, a pupil of Galileo. On Mount Puy de Dôme and at Clermont Cathedral, they were able to prove that atmospheric pressure diminished with increasing altitude. This meant that airless space—that is, space without matter— did exist. They had disproved the scientific and (at that time) theological thesis that "nature abhors a vacuum." Several years later Blaise became involved in a dispute over who had made this discovery first; his enthusiasm matched that of Galileo himself.

In 1648 Blaise Pascal returned to the study of mathematics. He wrote a Latin treatise on the measurement of conic sections (later used by Leibniz), and that same year reported on his experiments on the equilibrium of fluids.

52. René Descartes.
From a painting by Frans Hals.

PASCAL AND DESCARTES

An important encounter took place during this period. Pascal had two meetings with Descartes in Paris. The renowned mathematician and philosopher (born in La Haye, March 31, 1596) had heard a great deal about the young genius and was anxious to meet him. But the two learned men disagreed sharply about the existence of the vacuum. René Descartes, along with Francis Bacon in England, was one of the leading scientific minds of his day. He had founded analytical geometry, which deals with the measurement of geometrical bodies, and was also the first to formulate the modern theory of inertia: "Natural motions operate with uniform velocity on a straight line, not in a circle." This theorem contradicted Galileo's view that natural motions operate in a circle. Descartes dedicated himself to two main tasks: to construct a universal mathematical methodology, and to construct a mechanistic model of natural processes via this mathematical method.

What interests us here is the contrast between Descartes and Pascal. For Descartes, only three concepts were not accessible to the methodology of mathematics (which is still the case): motion, expansion, and the idea of God. He constructed a picture of a machine-like world from which the Creator had withdrawn. Pascal never forgave Descartes for entertaining and propounding this notion of a remote, unfeeling God. When Descartes died in Stockholm on February 11, 1650, Pascal did not lament his passing. He felt that Descartes had betrayed faith for the sake of science.

53. Title page of Descartes's chief work "Le Monde."

LE
MONDE
DE
Mᴿ DESCARTES,
ou
LE TRAITÉ DE LA
LVMIERE,
ET
DES AVTRES PRINCIPAVX
objets des Sens.

Avec un Discours du Mouvement Local, & un autre des Fièvres, composez selon les principes du mème Auteur.

A PARIS,
Chez THEODORE GIRAD, dans la Grand'
Salle du Palais, du cofté de la Cour des
Aydes, à l'Enuie.

M. DC. LXIV.
Avec Priuilege du Roy.

TRAITEZ
DE
L'EQVILIBRE
DES LIQVEVRS,
ET
DE LA PESANTEVR
DE LA
MASSE DE L'AIR.

Contenant l'explication des caufes de divers
effets de la nature, qui n'avoient point efté
bien connus jufques ici, particulierement
de ceux quel'on avoit attribuez à l'horreur
du Vuide.

Par Monfieur PASCAL.
SECONDE EDITION.

A PARIS,
En la Boutique de CHARLES SAVREUX.
Chez GVILLAUME DESPREZ, au
pied de la Tour de Nôtre-Dame du
côte de l'Archevêché.

M. DC. LXIV.
AVEC PRIVILEGE DV ROY.

*54. Title page from Pascal's treatise
on the weight of air.*

Pascal had not always felt that way, however. But when his conversion to Jansenism eventually came about, his fervor far exceeded that of his father, who had been converted in 1646, after falling in a slippery street during a frost, and fracturing his thigh. Two noblemen, brothers and gifted bone-setters, treated him for three months. They became guests at the Pascal home. These noblemen were Jansenists, and through them the Pascal family became acquainted with the writings of Cornelius Jansen (1585–1638), the former bishop of Ypres.

In 1640, soon after Bishop Jansen's death, a book of his on St. Augustine was published; it propounded certain teachings of Augustine that the Church had rejected—on predestination, man's corrupt will, and the irresistible power of God's grace. A sect gathered around Jansen, markedly opposed to the Jesuits and later condemned by the Church. Among the most vital aspects of Jansenist teaching were active love of one's neighbor and the practice of the Christian way of life.

Pascal was thirteen when his father came into contact with the Jansenists. Although the family did not join the group immediately, two years later they established contact with the convent of Port-Royal. Pascal's younger sister, Jacqueline, listened avidly to Jansenist preachers, and she was anxious to enter the convent. Her father opposed the move; and when he died in 1651, Blaise himself stood in her way. But she was persistent in her desire, and eventually entered Port-Royal despite his objections. For a while, Blaise and Jacqueline were estranged from one another.

While Jacqueline underwent this religious conversion, Blaise was living the life of a man of the world. According to his older sister's biography, he frequented the salons of Paris, accompanied pretty young women of noble birth, and undertook successful business ventures. In 1652 he sent one of his calculating machines to Queen Christina of Sweden. He wrote her a long letter of dedication in which he went so far as to compare scientists to monarchs. He had a reputation for intellectual pride. Two years later, the young Pascal renounced the world; he had suffered pain every day of his life from his nineteenth year.

THE CHOICE FOR GOD

In September 1654 Blaise reached a *rapprochement* with his younger sister at Port-Royal. On November 23 he had his spiritual experience. Soon afterwards he went to stay at Port-Royal. By this time, the Jansenist controversy was raging in France. Five theses of Jansen had been declared heretical. All five dealt with religious, not scientific questions.

Pascal now became an apologist for the Jansenist version of Christianity. Earlier, in 1647, he had been involved with a Jesuit in a debate over his theories on the vacuum. Now he became involved in the debates between Jansenists and Jesuits. He argued brilliantly, but he was on the losing side. Romano Guardini has noted that the Jansenists championed God's glory, whereas the Jesuits stood for man's freedom. Pascal, the scientist, opted for the former, upholding predestination and belief in miracles.

Pascal did not, however, renounce science, for he wrote another book on geometry for the disciples at Port-Royal, as well as a treatise on the properties of the cycloid; and he came close to formulating a modern theory of probability when he debated roulette with several other mathematicians.

After the death of his sister Jacqueline, who had been greatly upset by the raging controversy, Pascal left Port-Royal, and once again turned to worldly matters. One of his first projects was to establish the first municipal bus line in Paris, which began service on March 18, 1662. Soon afterwards, however, his health gave way completely. He spent his last months with Gilberte, who fought his desire to die among the poor in the Hospital for Incurables. After weeks of agony, he died in Paris on August 19, 1662. Two years after his death, the persecution of Jansenists began in earnest. Port-Royal was devastated in 1709.

55. Title page of Kircher's "Iter exstaticum Kircherianum" (1671). The learned Jesuit is depicted on the left.

THE EXISTENTIALIST

Pascal was an existentialist before his time. He tried to resolve man's relationship to the infinite, and in so doing he moved away from scientific research. Paul Valéry reproached him for tacking aphorisms to his clothing instead of inventing calculus. He left the latter problem to others.

But Pascal's decision must be respected. It is one possible response to a question of which he was fully aware, and which he tried to answer. As he put it, "In terms of the infinite (in the mathematical sense), all finite measures are the same. I see no reason why we should take a greater fancy to the latter than to the former. Only our accommodation to the finite makes us sad." Pascal came to regard man in terms of these relationships. Only a religious solution could be found for such perplexities.

In formulating this solution, Pascal did not reject a mathematical line of argument. Even his proof of God's existence is a form of probability theory. He offered to make a wager with unbelievers that there is a God and divine revelation. As he saw it, they had nothing to lose and everything to win by accepting that possibility. If infinity is nothing, then all our finite realities can add nothing to it; it, too, is nothing. Since we cannot prove or disprove God's existence for sure, we might as well treat it as a game of chance and place ourselves in God's hands. Pascal tried to show in many ways why this risk is worth taking.

No one had ever fought so strongly against the new revolution in scientific thought. But Pascal's fight was in vain. The rising tide of scientific ideas pushed forward. Mathematics and empirical research were not to be stopped.

56. Athanasius Kircher.

The scientific picture now began to take on new dimensions. No longer was it a matter of isolated individuals struggling against the whole world. The scientist no longer stood alone, out of touch with his colleagues in other countries. Galileo, for example, did not know his contemporary Sir Francis Bacon (1561–1626), who tried to introduce experimental methods into science around the same time. Nor was he familiar with the work of François Viéta (1540–1603), the founder of modern algebra, whose work was carried further by the English astronomer and mathematician Thomas Harriot.

During Galileo's lifetime, John Napier (1550–1617) and Henry Briggs (1556–1630) had discovered the logarithm; but only now was it becoming a common possession of all scientists. People could now enclose physical dimensions in mathematical equations, using specific and carefully chosen symbols. Team work entered the world of science. Scientists now began to work together on scientific problems.

Galileo's treatment by the Inquisition sent shock waves through Europe, creating a chasm between science and the Catholic Church that was to last for centuries. So strong was the impact that Descartes destroyed the finished manuscript of *Le Monde* when he heard of the Inquisition's verdict. Scientific endeavor now shifted its center to the Protestant nations of northwestern Europe: Switzerland, Holland, Germany, Scandinavia, and, in particular, England.

Only among the Jesuits were there any proponents of science in the Church. The versatile scholar Athanasius Kircher (1601–1680), seeking to find a mathematical base for his encyclopedic world view, tried to synthesize the knowledge of his time in a coherent whole, relying heavily on the findings of Jesuit missionaries throughout the world. Mathematics, it seemed to him, was the supreme unifying principle of natural phenomena. He was even more radical in this respect than Descartes: "The relationship between man, God, and the world is one of number," he wrote. "The soul measures external harmony by means of its own internal harmony. God is harmony in the loftiest sense; his calculations create the world."

Kircher also developed the concept of Pascal's calculating machine. He wanted to build a "logical machine" that could do every kind of thinking. In 1671 he was visited by young Wilhelm Leibniz (1646–1716), who was also interested in this project. Both had glimpsed the possibility of building what we now call a "computer." But the proper mathematical, technical, and engineering prerequisites were not yet at hand.

Scientific initiative became a hallmark of the Protestant world, and during this period no great scientist was Catholic. The more famous men of this time were, in Germany, the physicist Otto von Guericke (1602–1686); in Holland, Christian Huygens (1629–1695); in Denmark, Olaf Römer (1644–1710); and in England, John Wallis (1616–1703) and Isaac Newton.

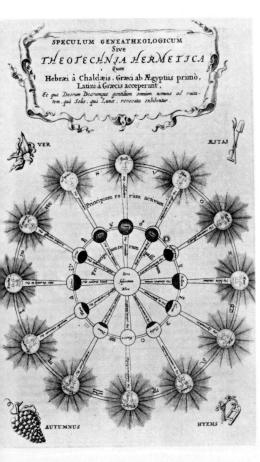

57. Illustration from Kircher's book 'Turris Babel'.

NEWTON

ISAAC NEWTON

Born: December 25, 1642, in Woolsthorpe

Died: March 20, 1727, in Kensington

"THAT THE PLANETS CAN BE KEPT IN THEIR ORBITS BY CENTRIPETAL FORCES IS EVIDENT FROM THE MOTION OF A PROJECTILE. A THROWN STONE, PROPELLED BY ITS OWN WEIGHT, IS DEFLECTED FROM A STRAIGHT-LINE COURSE, FOLLOWS A CURVE IN THE AIR, AND ULTIMATELY FALLS TO EARTH. IF IT IS THROWN WITH GREATER VELOCITY, IT WILL GO FARTHER. IT IS CONCEIVABLE THAT IF THE VELOCITY WERE INCREASED ENOUGH, THE STONE WOULD ULTIMATELY SHOOT BEYOND THE BORDERS OF EARTH AND NOT FALL BACK AGAIN."

Isaac Newton, describing the interaction of gravity and centrifugal force in his "On the System of the World", the third book of the *Principia Mathematica*.

The previous page shows a portrait of Newton from Trinity College, Cambridge.

Right: The locale of a famous legend, the garden of Newton's family home in Woolsthorpe. Here, on a summer evening in 1666, an apple is supposed to have fallen on his head, giving him the idea that the descent of a body on earth and the motion of celestial bodies are based on the same physical principle.

*Below: Newton built this bridge over a canal at Queen's College, Cambridge.
The bridge was designed so that all the beams would be self-supporting and would
not have to be nailed together.*

*Right: In his attempts to measure the speed of sound, Newton used
the echo in the Cloisters at Trinity College.*

Left: Newton's reflecting telescope, which he gave to the Royal Society. Alongside it is the extra reflector which he ground himself. To the left, his construction drawings.

Right: Under the portrait of his great predecessor, Galileo, Newton was knighted by Queen Anne in 1705 at the Master's Lodge in Trinity College.

Next page: Newton bought his first prism at a country market. With it he discovered the dispersion of white sunlight into the colors of the spectrum.

THE STARRY-EYED MECHANIC

Isaac Newton was the epitome of the modern scientist. He was keen-eyed and cool-headed in his scientific work, absent-minded where other things were concerned. Of course, he was involved in scientific disputes as were many of his predecessors. But they were academic disputes on scientific questions, devoid of rancor and personal chagrin. Newton never raised his voice or became heated; and no one ever heard him laugh out loud.

Like Copernicus, Newton preferred to hold back his work instead of forcing it on the world at large. He had already conceived his major ideas at the age of twenty-four, but it was years before he published the fully developed theories. Like Tycho Brahe, he continued perseveringly to gather data from his observations, and patiently to collate them over the years.

Therefore Newton seems to personify what was best in his great predecessors. He stood on the shoulders of giants, using the results obtained by Kepler, Galileo, and Descartes. And he himself was a giant in the field of intellectual endeavor. He knew how to discern the most important ideas in the mass of data handed down from others.

Newton, like Kepler, was a believing Christian who saw no conflict between faith and scientific research. Like Galileo, he was a superb mechanic who could build fine instruments for himself. Like Descartes and Pascal, he was a mathematician; he used the new discoveries in mathematics to express his problems in quantitative form, and to work out a solution.

But Newton, unlike his predecessors, took the notion of scientific co-operation very seriously. He did not display his work to win applause or adulation. He communicated his results in order to obtain the reaction of other scientists and to inspire similar efforts on their part. He wanted others to correct his own work. Unlike his predecessors, Newton was free of the older, dogmatic tendencies.

FROM SHEPHERD-BOY TO PROFESSOR

Isaac Newton was born in the year of Galileo's death. He grew up in Woolsthorpe, a village in Lincolnshire, where his mother had a meager property. Like Pascal he was a sickly child, and the neighbors felt he would not survive. But his mother and grandmother did everything they could to keep him alive, and they succeeded. Newton's mother was widowed at an early age, and her life was hard. Her eldest son, Isaac, was expected to shoulder some of her burden, but he was a failure in this respect.

Left: Christopher Wren, one of the great seventeenth-century architects, built Greenwich Observatory. The zero meridian runs through the center of the octagonal room. Newton and Halley often came to Greenwich to observe the stars with Flamsteed, the Astronomer Royal. The ladder at the right was used to adjust the height of the telescope.

Like the young Pascal, Newton was thoughtful and mechanically inclined. As a boy, he invented a moving vehicle that was operated by a pedal. A sundial, which he himself constructed, decorated the family home. At sixteen, he built a water meter. He was always busy on some sort of construction work. He read a great deal and was also a good draughtsman.

It was a different story when it came to sheep-herding. The flock would wander off while Isaac sat to one side in deep thought. At the end of the day someone else would have to round up the sheep. On one occasion all the sheep were accounted for, but Isaac himself was missing. After a long search they found him lost in thought over some problem in conics.

Isaac was, first and foremost, a staunch and tireless observer. One day in 1658 a frightful storm broke. People were terrified as roofs were torn off, fields uprooted, and tides rose. But on that very day Isaac measured the velocity of the wind, devising his own distinctive method. He knew that he could jump seven feet on his own power. With the wind blowing against him, he could not get anywhere. With the wind at his back, he could jump fourteen feet. Knowing the surface area of his own body and using his own broadjump mark as a constant, he worked out the pushing force of the wind. The whole experiment was carefully planned and executed.

Despite her poverty, his mother resolved that Isaac would get a good education. His stepfather, rector of the next parish, came to her aid and helped to pay the costs involved. Isaac attended a good school in Grantham, where other famous men of his day began their education. Sir William Cecil, an adviser to Queen Elizabeth, attended the same school. After attending grammar school, Newton studied under a well-known chemist and pharmacist named Clark. He lived with the Clark family until he was eighteen, taking full advantage of Clark's excellent library. He fell in love, for the first and last time in his life, with Clark's stepdaughter. But the absent-minded Newton never thought to propose to her, and she eventually married someone else. They remained good friends, however.

At the age of 18, Newton arrived at Cambridge University. He enrolled at Trinity College, which was founded by Henry VIII in 1546. Many famous statesmen, churchmen, and scholars, including Francis Bacon, had preceded him there.

Newton's preparatory training was somewhat behind that of his classmates, but he soon caught up with them. He undertook the study of analytical geometry, and his tutor instructed him to study Kepler's book on optics. In 1663 Newton began to study under Isaac Barrow, a distinguished theologian and mathematician, whose favorite pupil he soon became. Barrow regarded mathematics as the basic science, even of theology; his personal and scholarly influence on the young Newton was enormous. The fatherless student came to look upon him as his spiritual father.

Because of his modesty, reserve, and detachment, Newton did not make a deep impression on anyone at the start. As time went on, however, he won more and more friends and was favorably regarded by all. His absent-mindedness soon became legendary at the college. Lost in concentration, he would not hear the dinner-bell ring: his classmates would have to drag him to the supper table. It is recorded that

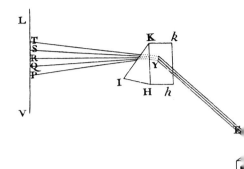

58. *Newton's diagram of his experiment with prisms. The light ray (O) comes from the right (F), passes through a crack in the darkened room and strikes the prism (ABC), where it is broken up. The color band (pqrst) is reunified in the lens (MN) and reflected as white light onto the prism (DEG). Another prism (HIK) breaks up this white light, identical with (O), again into a spectral band (TSRQP). The experiment showed that "natural" white light is broken up into the spectrum exactly the same as "artificial" white light that is put together from the spectral color bands.*

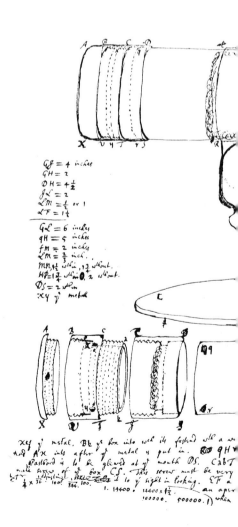

130

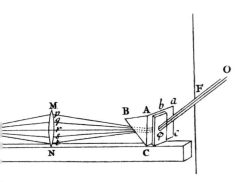

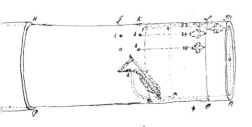

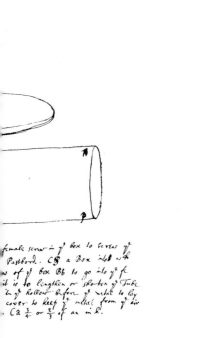

59. Newton's diagram of his telescope and its parts. The idea of using mirrors in a telescope was not new, but the difficulties entailed in putting together the proper reflecting surface discouraged its practical execution. Newton was the first to attempt to put together the proper reflecting surface, and he polished the mirror himself.

others would wager whether he would show up or not. When he had solved a particularly vexing problem, he would eat with great relish.

Newton made rapid progress. In 1664, four years after his entrance, he was made a scholar. In 1665 he took his B. A. In 1667 he took his Master's degree, and became a Fellow of Trinity College. He was now entitled to receive an allotted stipendium, so that his family was relieved of the financial burden. In 1669 Professor Barrow freely surrendered his chair to his favorite pupil. Newton, at the age of twenty-seven, officially became what he had always been: the learned professor, totally absorbed in his work.

Barrow's gesture was a moving spectacle, and it says something about the spirit of this new generation of scientists. He himself was only forty when he surrendered his chair to Newton. Yet he willingly stepped aside for his pupil and friend, whose mind was soaring ahead. At some cost to himself, he returned to theology and pastoral work. Soon, however, he was made court chaplain; three years later, in 1672, he became Master of Trinity College.

A REFLECTING TELESCOPE

The year he received his appointment, Newton built the first reflecting telescope. He made every bit of the instrument himself. A movable sphere, held by two springs, is fastened to a plate, so that the telescope tube can be turned to any desired position. The incoming light rays are brought into focus through a concave mirror. From there a small tilted mirror reflects them onto the eyepiece, which contains a powerful magnifying lens. Even the alloy of the mirror was Newton's own discovery; and he himself polished the mirror.

Newton built this reflecting telescope to eliminate the chromatic distortion that occurred in the existing lens telescope. Yet he himself did not undertake many stellar observations. His main concern was to get precise results from those who did observe the stars, so that he could use accurate data for his own calculations.

Newton had already done his first important research on the spectrum. At twenty-four he had investigated the dispersion of light rays into the primary colors. He went down many blind alleys, and did not feel satisfied with his results. He wanted to work out his findings mathematically before publishing them. It is only in 1671 that he alluded to his discoveries in a letter.

In 1671 Newton exhibited his telescope at the Royal Society where it was examined by Charles II. In 1672 Newton described his researches on spectral dispersion to the Royal Society and in that year he was elected a Fellow of the Society.

THE ROYAL SOCIETY

Of all the scholarly societies devoted to scientific and technical advancement, the Royal Society has made the greatest contributions. Founded in 1660, its membership increased from one hundred to two hundred in the first ten years of its existence. It was composed of eight committees, each representing a different area of specialization. The field of mechanics was most strongly represented — with sixty-nine members. The business trades had thirty-five representatives, while agriculture boasted thirty-two representatives. The discipline of astronomy had only fifteen members, but that was a fair amount for a purely academic discipline.

The ideas of Francis Bacon were the prime inspiration behind the establishment of this society. In his *New Atlantis,* Bacon had portrayed a scientific, scholarly academy which he described as a "Salomon's House." It was not to be simply a forum for scholarly lectures but an experimental center with laboratories, workshops, and libraries. The knowledge obtained from these experiments was to be codified in encyclopedias. As Bacon put it, "the goal is to seek out the underlying principles of things and their hidden motion, and to extend man's capacity for accomplishment in all these areas."

This basic aim was adopted in the statutes of the Royal Society. In 1663 Robert Hooke, Professor of Mechanics to the Royal Society, said that the aim and purpose of the Royal Society was to improve, through experimentation, knowledge of natural realities and all useful arts, manufacturing methods, mechanical processes, machines, and inventions (steering clear of theology, metaphysics, ethics, politics, grammar, rhetoric, and logic); to retrieve any useful art or invention that may have fallen into disuse; to test all relevant systems, theories, principles, hypotheses, and other data of ancient and modern authors, in order to formulate a comprehensive and sound philosophical system explaining natural phenomena and uncovering the underlying rationale of things.

Noteworthy is the fact that here, for the first time, we find expressed an ideological tie up between business, trade, industry, agriculture, and science. Many members of the Society were not only scientists and scholars but also businessmen. This original outlook, envisioning the practical application of scientific data, began to fade into the background around Newton's time. A Galilean tendency began to take hold, and thus Newton's ideas fell on fertile soil. His ideas were widely discussed, within the Royal Society and elsewhere.

THE DISPUTE WITH LEIBNIZ

Newton did not escape the problem of scientific squabbling and quarrels over the primacy in scientific discovery. These arguments proved to be storms in a teacup later on, but they did upset him at the time; Newton himself had no desire to get involved in them.

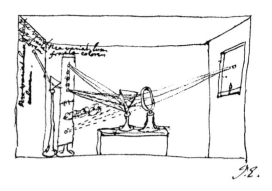

60. Newton's diagram on the dispersion of light in passing through a prism. Newton himself tells us that while he was quarantined in Woolsthorpe (1665–1666) because of the plague, he made his three most important discoveries: 1) the law of gravity, 2) the nature of white light (see sketch 58), and 3) the infinitesimal calculus. The historian can tell us little as to how Newton made these discoveries; his aversion to publicity is well known.

61. Gottfried Wilhelm Leibniz. From a sketch made in 1714.

NEWTON:
GRAVITATION AND SPECTRUM

THE LAW OF GRAVITATION

Both Copernicus and Kepler had suspected the existence of some such force as gravity. Gradually, astronomers became convinced that some comprehensive principle had to be behind Kepler's three laws. We do not know how Newton arrived at his law of gravitation and thus formulated the connecting link. His magnum opus does not tell us what his starting point was. Did he find a bridge between Galilei's law of free fall and Kepler's laws of planetary motion?

It is a moot question whether Newton himself found the connection between the laws of circular motion and centripetal force (Huygens' work) on the one hand, and Kepler's third law of planetary motion on the other. But if we put those two laws together, it necessarily follows that the centrifugal force of two planets is inversely proportional to the square of their distance from the sun. Now, according to Galileo, force and mass match each other. Newton himself formulated the principle (action versus reaction) that the sun is attracted by each planet with the same force that it exerts on that planet. All this led him to formulate another fundamental law: *Two bodies attract each other with a force that is directly proportional to their mass, and inversely proportional to the square of the distance between them.*

Using this law of attraction, Newton now sought to calculate the force which kept the moon in its orbit and prevented it from flying off on a tangent. He then compared this with the force exerted on a stone during free fall, as indicated by Galileo's experiments. The results proved disappointing. The correlation was short by 20%, because Newton had to use the existing figure for the radius of earth. Disappointed, Newton put his work aside. It was 1666.

In 1671 and 1684 the French astronomer Picard published his new earth measurements. The older value of 297,251 Parisian feet for a 1 degree of arc of the earth's surface was replaced by a value of 342,360 feet. Thus the value of the earth's radius was raised correspondingly. Newton saw at once that new figure would establish the correlation he had been looking for. His hypothesis had been correct: gravitation was a universal characteristic of matter. Every planet is attracted by the sun in direct proportion to its mass and in inverse proportion to the square of its distance from the sun.

In his two years of intense work, Newton used his newly developed calculus to prove that Kepler's three laws necessarily followed from his law of gravitation. To be specific, he showed that on the basis of his law the orbital path of a body, whose gravitational center was the sun, had to be conic (a circle, ellipse, parabola, or

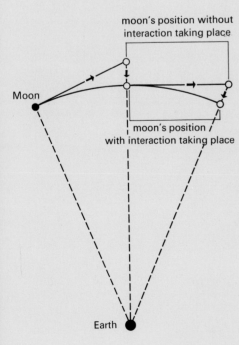

Newton saw the moon's orbit as a continuous process of interaction. By segmenting the moon's orbit as shown in this diagram, he was able to calculate the gravitational attraction exerted on it by the earth.

moon's position without
interaction taking place

Moon

moon's position
with interaction taking place

Earth

hyperbola). This provided an exact scientific explanation for many hitherto inexplicable phenomena: planetary and lunar motion, the ellipticity of the earth, peculiarities in the motion of the earth's axis (precession), the ebb and flow of tides, etc.

Newton's findings are contained in his three-volume work, *Philosophiae naturalis principia mathematica*. It is often remarked that Newton's *Principia* remade the face of science, and there is much truth in that. In this work we find, among other things, the three famous axioms that form the basis of Newtonian mechanics:

1. A body remains in a state of rest or of uniform motion in a straight line unless acted upon by an external force.
2. A change in momentum is proportional to the force causing the change.
3. To every action there is always an equal and opposite, or contrary, reaction.

Newton's *Principia* laid the foundation for present-day science. Newtonian mechanics, rooted in a series of carefully formulated axioms, became the model for scientific disciplines that arose later. Two hundred years later, two concepts in this closed system were the starting-point for another leap forward by physics. Albert Einstein successfully challenged Newton's notion that *time* and *space* were absolutes.

WORK ON THE SPECTRUM

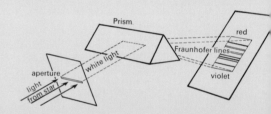

A prism separates white light into its constituent colors (wave lengths).

Newton's investigations into the nature of light were just as significant. He pioneered new techniques for the study of the cosmos. Galileo's use of a refracting telescope and Newton's construction of a reflecting telescope enabled men to gather a larger quantity of light from the outside cosmos. And Newton's study of light dispersion in the spectrum paved the way for further study of the quality of starlight. In 1859 Gustav Kirchhoff (1824–1887) and Robert Bunsen (1811–1899) inaugurated spectrum analysis.

In his classic experiments Newton proved that "white" light is broken up into the colors of the rainbow when it is directed through an aperture onto a prism. He also proved that this dispersed light could be recombined as white light, and that the process could be repeated over again (see pictures pp. 130–132).

Light from different colors has different wave lengths. The "angstrom unit" is the standard unit of measurement. 1 angstrom = 0.0000001 mm.

In another fundamental experiment Newton proved that the resultant colors could not be broken up further. From this he concluded that "white" light is composed of homogeneous (monochromatic) color components, and that these components are clearly split up in a prism. Newton's work challenged many existing theories about the nature of light, but we shall consider the later impact of Newton's pioneer work for astronomy.

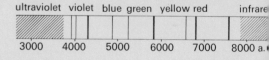

Newton had used sunlight for his spectral experiments. It soon became clear that the light of other incandescent bodies could be broken up into a spectrum. Gustav Kirchhoff and Robert Bunsen discovered that all incandescent solids and liquids under high pressure produce continuous spectra like the one Newton obtained

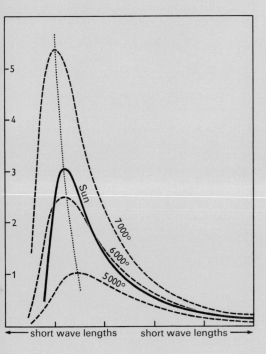

The hotter a body is, the more the peak of its radiation intensity (the dotted line) lies at the short wave end of the spectrum.

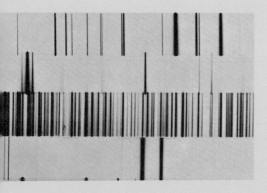

Every chemical element is recognizable by the lines in its spectrum. The picture shows the spectra (from top to bottom) of tin, copper, iron, and aluminum.

The sun is a medium-size star. The diagram shows its relationship to the attributes of other stars. The sun values are set at one (shaded line).

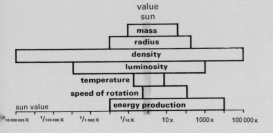

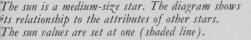

from sunlight. Later it was discovered that the energy distribution in a given spectrum depended upon the temperature of the radiating body. Astronomy could now take a major step forward, using spectroscopic analysis to determine the temperature of a star.

SPECTROSCOPIC ANALYSIS

Upon closer study of solar and stellar spectrums, Joseph Fraunhofer (1787–1826) discovered that many dark lines were present in them. Bunsen and Kirchhoff later concluded that these dark lines appeared when gaseous bodies were involved. Moreover, every chemical element of a gaseous nature produced its own distinctive set of spectral lines. Thus the presence of a given set of lines indicated, with absolute certainty, the presence of a particular chemical element.

Spectroscopic theory has made giant strides since its beginnings. From the general appearance and quality of spectral lines we can now say a great deal about the environment which emits these lines: its temperature, pressure, magnetic fields, motion, and chemical makeup. Here we shall not go into the difference between bright lines and dark absorption lines in spectrum analysis.

SPECTRUM ANALYSIS OF THE STARS

Countless thousands of star spectra have been subjected to close analysis. Here we shall briefly touch upon some of the more important findings.

1. In contrast to the moon and planets illuminated by the sun, stars are extremely hot balls of gas emitting their own light. Their surface temperature may well exceed 100,000 degrees. In general we may say that the bluer the color of a star, the hotter it is; if the color is more yellow or red, the star is cooler. Temperature differences are registered in the stellar spectra, and thus we can classify stars according to their spectral type.

2. Using general laws of physics and spectral analysis, we can say some general things about the makeup of these stars. They are of such great mass that the inward-directed force of gravitation in these bodies is exactly balanced by the outward-directed force of gas pressure and radiation pressure. (Radiation, including light, exerts pressure.) As a result, we can conclude that temperatures of over a million degrees are to be found in the interior of the stars, along with enormous pressures and densities.

3. Spectral analysis indicates that almost all the matter in the universe is composed of hydrogen and helium. The relative mixture is 57% hydrogen, 40% helium, and 3% all other chemical elements; this mixture prevails almost unchanged throughout the universe. The high temperatures, densities, and pressures in the interior of the stars give rise to a whole series of nuclear fission processes, releasing energy that comes to us in the form of heat, light, radio waves, and X-rays.

4. On the basis of general physical principles, astrophysics can tell us something about the constitution of the stars. There is a close interrelation between the basic factors that go to make a star (i.e. its mass, radius, density, luminosity, temperature, speed of rotation, and energy production). Its luminosity, for example, is tied up with its surface temperature. If we plot this interrelationship we obtain the diagram to the right, which depicts the various stages of stellar development.

Knowing that transformations take place in the interior of a star (e.g. hydrogen is transformed into helium), we no longer regard the stars as fixed, unchanging entities. They do undergo development. The nova phenomenon, which Tycho Brahe observed, is probably a very late stage in stellar development which some stars go through once.

The interrelationship of a star's mass and luminosity is another important piece of information which has told us much about gaseous stars.

5. Close study of a star's spectral lines reveals typical patterns of splitting, expansion, and shifting in relation to their normal configuration. From this we can make deductions about the star's rotation on its axis, the strength of its magnetic field, and gas turbulence in its atmosphere. On the basis of the Doppler effect (see page 23*), we can also determine whether it is moving towards the earth or away from it.

When we put together everything we know about the heavenly bodies, we find a surprising situation. We actually know much more about the distant fixed stars than we do about the nearby planets. This is so because we get much direct information about the stars, particularly about their outer atmosphere, from their spectra. In studying the planets, however, we must use the reflected solar spectrum, which does not provide too much specific information about the planets.

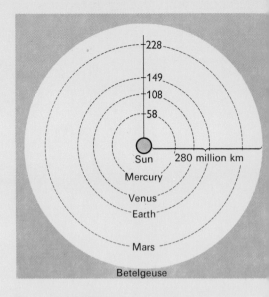

Stars are giant balls of gas. The red giant stars — Betelgeuse in Orion is depicted here — are so large that large portions of our solar system could fit into them. The sun is scaled disproportionately large in this drawing.

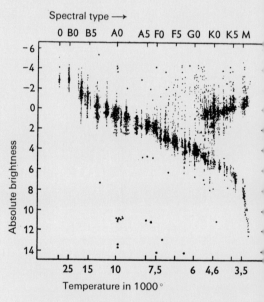

The Hertzsprung-Russell Diagram for the stars in the vicinity of the sun. Each point represents a star with that absolute brightness and spectral type (temperature).

From the width of their spectral lines, astronomers know that Vega rotates much slower than Atair.

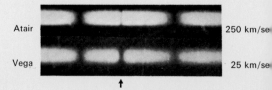

The bitterest dispute was with Leibniz, the German philosopher, who was Newton's only peer in mathematics. It started in 1673, when Leibniz visited England. He came upon a manuscript of Newton, in which the young student had set down his ideas on mathematical integration and the infinitesimal calculus. Who had discovered these things first? The argument then begun was carried on bitterly for many years.

At first it would seem that this dispute ran counter to the growing spirit of co-operation among scientists. But the interesting thing is that Leibniz did not want to get involved in an argument either. The whole debate was really initiated by friends of these two scholars. A second-rate publication appeared, picturing Newton as a pupil of Leibniz. Later, in fact, Leibniz did indirectly accuse Newton of plagiarism. Newton was persuaded by his friends to write a reply. His friends in the Royal Society published it, and it asserted that Leibniz was a plagiarist. Today we know that the two men were working on the same problem independently, and that they arrived at the same results around the same time.

One interesting aspect of the dispute is that many scholars lined up on one side or the other. The Royal Society backed Newton, while Leibniz was supported by the Swiss mathematicians, Jakob (1654–1705) and Johann Bernoulli (1667–1748). Other scientists, such as Huygens, tried to mediate between the two sides.

SUCCESS AFTER SUCCESS

Despite such debates, Newton's life ran smoothly and quietly. It was a long journey from farm boy to professor, and one not easily made. Yet Newton moved onward and upward without encountering great obstacles. He made many friends among his pupils. One of them, the future Lord Halifax, greatly helped his later career.

In 1689 Newton was elected to the House of Commons. In 1696 Lord Halifax appointed him Warden of the Royal Mint. His qualifications as a chemist, particularly in the field of alloys, helped him to win this post. In 1699 he was appointed Master of the Mint. In 1703 Newton became president of the Royal Society, and he held this post until his death. The Society was jokingly referred to as "Sir Isaac's Parliament." In 1705 Newton was knighted by Queen Anne. He lived in London, built his own observatory, and occupied a palace which was run by his step-niece. He frequented the court of George I, where he was held in high esteem.

On March 20, 1727, at the age of eighty-five, Newton died. His body was laid out in the Jerusalem chamber, and it was then borne to Westminster Abbey by royal pall-bearers. He was laid to rest among kings and bishops.

62. Letter of Halley to Newton about his book "Principia mathematica." Halley urged Newton to write it, and he even bore the printing costs.

Like the other founders of modern science, Newton was sure his work would bring him nearer to the Creator of the world. He wished to investigate and discover not only the material data of the universe but the Infinite as well. But he did not share Descartes's conviction that the world was a machine set in motion by God and then left to itself. As he put it: "The true God continues to exist and is present everywhere. He exists always and everywhere, he fashions space and duration."

Newton regarded space, time, and motion as absolutes permeated by an ethereal medium that proceeds from God. He could say with deep conviction: "When I was formulating my work on the universe, my attention was drawn to principles that could inspire belief in a divine being. Nothing could give me greater pleasure than to see that it was serviceable in this respect."

For many years Newton brooded over the connection between gravity and centrifugal force. He was not able to provide a satisfactory explanation of either force, but he did discover their interrelationship. By collating Kepler's work on the moon's orbit with Galileo's work on the trajectory of a projectile, he came to realize that the elliptical orbit of a planet resulted from the interaction of gravity and centrifugal force. In his "On the System of the World", the third book of the *Principia*, he described how he arrived at this conclusion.

Newton began to ponder this problem at the age of twenty-four, but he was forty-four before he managed to formulate his theory. The formulation was his own, but many other scientists helped him to arrive at it. Of particular importance were the careful measurements of the earth's size by French scientists. Their measurements gave him valuable data. The English physicist, Robert Hooke (1635–1703), introduced the notion that "ether" transmitted light. Edmund Halley, the astronomer, was a close friend of Newton, and he discussed many of his own problems with him. It was Halley who persuaded Newton to prepare his work for publication. When, in 1686, Newton could not publish his *Principia mathematica* for lack of money, Halley paid the printing costs. This spirit of teamwork, evinced by highly individualistic men, was something new in the history of science. In itself it was a major breakthrough for sience.

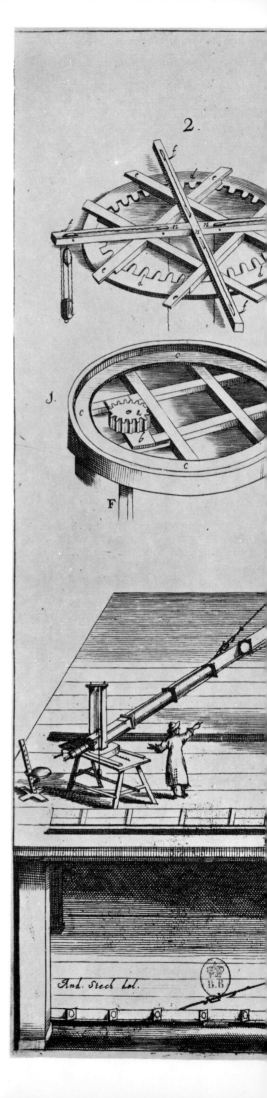

63. Sketch of a multi-lens telescope. Such telescopes became bigger and bigger in the second half of the seventeenth century. Lengths of 100 feet or more were not uncommon. These lengths were necessary to overcome various optical flaws, such as chromatic distortion.

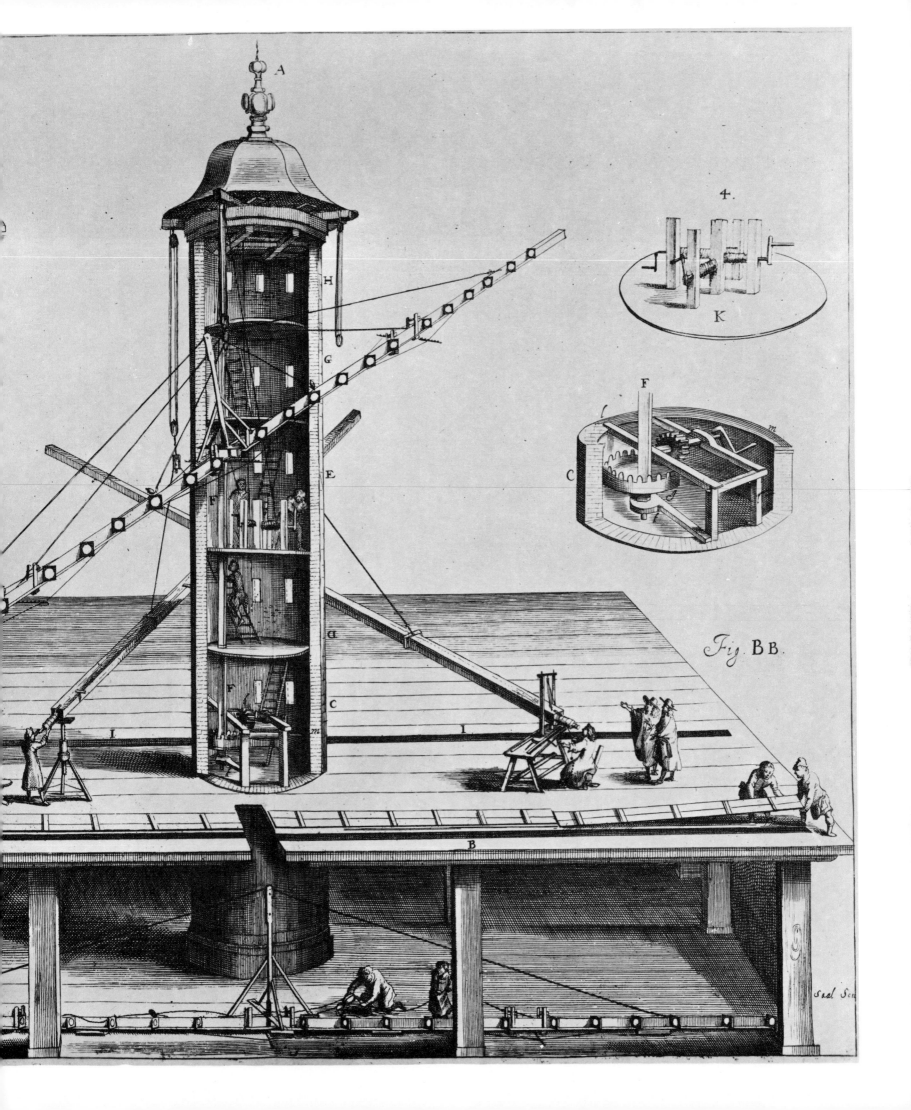

Fig. BB.

FROM NEWTON TO EINSTEIN

With Newton astronomy passed once and for all into the modern age. Modern astronomy had taken shape. The solar system was viewed as a unified, closed system, governed by clear and simple laws. Various bodies revolved harmoniously around some central star — the planets around the sun, the moons of Jupiter around Jupiter — just as Copernicus had imagined. The enigma of the universe appeared to have been solved. Now scientists could deepen and expand this data.

But the new theory was not yet universally accepted. Objections were still raised by the forces of religion. Even in England some saw a threat to religion in these scientific theories. Bishop Berkely (1685–1753) asked, in 1734, whether mathematicians did not submit to authority and accept things on faith. He once said that it was beneath the dignity of the spirit to look for extreme precision in reducing individual phenomena to general laws or deducing the former from the latter. But the English mathematicians, who had taken issue with Berkeley, were soon able to show further progress in their work. In 1742 Colin MacLaurin offered an incontestable basis for differential calculus — the matter which had been under dispute.

64. *Leonard Euler.*

65. *Olaf Römer.*

MEASURING THE VELOCITY OF LIGHT

Many contemporaries of Newton helped to fill in the new picture of the universe, as did later scientists. Around 1675 the Danish astronomer, Olaf Römer (1644–1710), observed the moons of Jupiter and their regular eclipses. He also noticed that these eclipses occurred belatedly when earth and Jupiter moved farther away from each other. When the two planets moved closer to each other again, there was no delay in the eclipses. On the basis of this data, Römer managed to make a correct estimate of the velocity of light (186,000 miles per second).

Expeditions to various parts of the world during the eighteenth century brought new data, which confirmed Newton's theory on the flattening of the earth. Differential calculus, discovered by Newton and Leibniz, was further developed by the Bernoulli brothers in Basle and the German, Leonhard Euler (1707–1783). Two Frenchmen, Joseph Louis de Lagrange (1736–1813) and Pierre Simon de Laplace (1749–1827), also made important contributions to the new theories. Most importantly, they showed that deviations and disturbances in the solar system were compensated for within the system itself. Newton had assumed that God had to make corrections on a regular basis.

Pierre Simon de Laplace collated all the previous investigations of planetary motion since Newton, in particular the important work of Euler and Lagrange. These two scientists had investigated the disturbances in a planet's motion caused by the attraction of another planet. In general, Newton's law of gravity provided mathematical proof for the law of motion governing the interaction of only two bodies; but in astronomy more than two bodies are interacting. The multi-body problem could not be expressed in compact mathematical form. Lagrange discovered and solved some of the exceptional cases—the only ones to date.

In his famous work, *Mécanique céleste (Celestial Mechanics)*, Laplace provided a mathematical approach for dealing with a third body. He was also able to show that stability pervaded the solar system, and that the system had existed throughout a long period of astronomic time. As he noted: "By virtue of the fact that the motions of the planets and their satellites are almost circular, that they do not drift in any particular direction and do lie in relatively similar planes, the system oscillates around a midpoint from which it deviates only slightly." This led him to the conviction that the solar system could not have arisen by chance. He suggested that the whole solar system originated from a hot rotating mass of gas; and that rings had broken off from this mass to form the planets.

The great philosopher Immanuel Kant (1724–1804) formulated a similar theory. Today it is often called the Kant-Laplace theory, even though there was no direct connection between the two formulations. Kant started with the theory of an Englishman, Thomas Wright, who conjectured that the sun and the stars of the Milky Way moved within a gigantic system that had a common center. Taking this as his starting point, Kant proposed that a disordered mass of small particles had coalesced to form the celestial spheres.

66. Pierre Simon Laplace.

67. Friedrich Wilhelm Herschel.

HERSCHEL AND THE COSMIC NEBULAE

Friedrich Wilhelm Herschel (1738–1822), the outstanding astronomer at the turn of the century, made similar speculations. As an oboist in the Hanoverian Guards, he went to England and stayed there. He was particularly adept at grinding and polishing mirrors, and he built the first large reflecting telescope. Compared to the existing instruments, it was a giant telescope. In 1781 he enlarged our knowledge of the solar system by discovering the planet Uranus.

Herschel began a systematic study of the northern sky, dividing it up into specific sections and scrutinizing it very carefully. He discovered that the sun and all its planets moved in relation to the other stars. Of great importance were his star counts. They showed that the Milky Way had a lens-shaped form, and this agreed with Kant's view on the shape of nebulae.

For the ancients, the region of fixed stars had been a rigid, crystalline body housing

the Divine. Now it could be viewed as an enormous expanse, in which revolved gigantic bodies that dwarfed our own planetary system. Human standards of measurement and distance were no longer adequate. Scientists began to measure stellar distance in light years—the distance travelled by light in one year (at 186,000 miles per second). The figure is about 5.87 million million miles. The Andromeda nebula, similar in size to our Milky Way, is estimated to be over two million light years from earth.

Improvements in instruments and refinements in methodology during the nineteenth century brought further insights into external galaxies. By examining the positional change of the earth in its yearly revolution around the sun, scientists were able to measure the distance to the fixed stars. In 1838 the first such measurements were made by Friedrich Wilhelm Bessel (1784–1846) and Wilhelm Struve (1793–1864).

68. The giant reflecting telescope of F. W. Herschel, built between 1785 and 1789. Its focal length came to 39 feet. The reflector aperture was about 4 feet. The reflector, which King George III paid for, weighed more than a ton. Herschel used this monstrous instrument rarely. It was too cumbersome, and adaptations to temperature changes between night and day took so long that optical distortion occurred.

Knowledge of our own planetary system also progressed far in the nineteenth century. We could go so far as to say that the basic condition of the traditional planets was fully established, to the extent that this was possible by telescopic observation. In 1846 the planet Neptune was discovered. A little belatedly, in 1930, Pluto was added to the planetary scheme.

BODE'S LAW

	Distance Calculated	Real
Mercury	0 + 4 = 4	3.9
Venus	3 + 4 = 7	7.2
Earth	6 + 4 = 10	10.0
Mars	12 + 4 = 16	15.2
	24 + 4 = 28	
Jupiter	48 + 4 = 52	52.0
Saturn	96 + 4 = 100	95.5
Uranus	192 + 4 = 196	192.2
Neptune	—	301.1
Pluto	384 + 4 = 388	394.6

Bode's law in its present form. The reason for positing a gap between Mars and Jupiter is obvious. The planetoids filled this gap. The distance between the earth and the sun was arbitrarily fixed at 10.0 (see "real" distance column). Kepler, too, was interested in regularities of this sort, as is clear from his theory of platonic spheres.

69. Carl Friedrich Gauss.

PLUGGING THE GREAT GAP

The director of the Berlin Observatory, Johann Ehlert Bode (1747–1826), and his contemporary, David Titius (1729–1796), formulated a mathematical rule describing the distance between the planetary orbits. The formula indicated that there was an inexplicable "gap" between the orbits of Mars and Jupiter. Scientists conjectured that there must be another undiscovered planet lying between them.

On the night of January 2, 1801, the Italian astronomer Giuseppe Piazzi discovered a new star. He took it for a comet at first, because it was small and difficult to keep track of. But he managed to fix its position and to follow its course every night up to February 11. Then bad weather set in, and observation became impossible. Piazzi had forwarded news of his find to other observatories, including the Berlin Observatory, where Bode worked. Bode immediately conjectured that the new star was the lost planet between Mars and Jupiter.

The mysterious star was now lost in a bleak sky, but not Piazzi's information. Scholars and scientists in various disciplines began to collaborate on the new data. In Brunswick, Carl Friedrich Gauss (1777–1855), a twenty-four-year-old mathematician, heard of the discovery and obtained Piazzi's data. Using his own mathematical methodology, designed to pinpoint planetary orbits on the basis of a few observations, he was able to predict the course of the mysterious star. Scientific calculation had won another victory. The first night that the planet was sought, it was found right where Gauss said it would be. The name of this planetoid, the first to be discovered, is Ceres.

In subsequent years, a host of planetoids were found in the gap between Mars and Jupiter. Amateur and professional astronomers were caught up in the search for new stellar bodies. Approximately 2,000 such planetoids were discovered. The astronomer Palisa himself discovered 60. The larger planetoids, such as Ceres, are around 400 miles in diameter; but most of them are much smaller, more akin to meteorites. The general assumption is that planetoids are fragments of a large planet that broke off in the early history of the planetary system; but other explanations are also offered.

Heute endlich sollst Du mit mir zufrieden sein. Ich freue mich sehr über das grosse Interesse, das Du der Sache widmest. Ich stütze mich gar nicht auf die Arbeiten, sondern rechne Dir alles vor. Sollte dann immer noch etwas unverständlich bleiben, so kann die Lücke leicht ausgefüllt werden. —

1) Lagrange'sche Form der Gleichungen.

Behauptung: Es sei $\sqrt{-g} = 1$. Ausserdem sei $L = g^{\sigma\tau} \left\{ \begin{matrix} \sigma\,\beta \\ \alpha \end{matrix} \right\} \left\{ \begin{matrix} \tau\,\alpha \\ \beta \end{matrix} \right\}$. Dann ist, wenn L als Funktion der $g^{\sigma\tau}$ und $g^{\sigma\tau}_\alpha = \frac{\partial g^{\sigma\tau}}{\partial x_\alpha}$ aufgefasst wird:

$$\frac{\partial L}{\partial g^{\sigma\tau}} = -\left\{ \begin{matrix} \sigma\,\beta \\ \alpha \end{matrix} \right\}\left\{ \begin{matrix} \iota\,\alpha \\ \beta \end{matrix} \right\} \qquad \left.\begin{matrix} \\ \\ \\ \end{matrix}\right\} (1)$$

$$\frac{\partial L}{\partial g^{\sigma\tau}_\alpha} = -\left\{ \begin{matrix} \sigma\,\lambda \\ \alpha \end{matrix} \right\}$$

Bemerkung. Summationszeichen lasse ich immer weg. Über einen Index ist stets zu summieren, wenn er zweimal auftritt.

Beweis. Durch Differenziation von L folgt — immer als Funkt. von $g^{\sigma\tau} = g^{\sigma\tau}_\alpha$ betrachtet. folgt

$$dL = \left\{ \begin{matrix} \sigma\,\beta \\ \alpha \end{matrix} \right\}\left\{ \begin{matrix} \tau\,\alpha \\ \beta \end{matrix} \right\} dg^{\sigma\tau} + 2 g^{\sigma\tau}\left\{ \begin{matrix} \sigma\,\beta \\ \alpha \end{matrix} \right\} d\left\{ \begin{matrix} \tau\,\alpha \\ \beta \end{matrix} \right\} \qquad \Big(\text{Zwei nur durch die Benennung der Indizes verschiedene Glieder sind zusammengefasst}\Big)$$

Hieraus folgt weiter wegen $g^{\sigma\tau} d\left\{ \begin{matrix} \tau\,\alpha \\ \beta \end{matrix} \right\} = d\left(g^{\sigma\tau} \left\{ \begin{matrix} \tau\,\alpha \\ \beta \end{matrix} \right\}\right) - \left\{ \begin{matrix} \tau\,\alpha \\ \beta \end{matrix} \right\} dg^{\sigma\tau}$

$$dL = -dg^{\sigma\tau} \cdot \left\{ \begin{matrix} \sigma\,\beta \\ \alpha \end{matrix} \right\}\left\{ \begin{matrix} \tau\,\alpha \\ \beta \end{matrix} \right\} + 2\left\{ \begin{matrix} \sigma\,\beta \\ \alpha \end{matrix} \right\} d\left(g^{\sigma\tau}\left\{ \begin{matrix} \tau\,\alpha \\ \beta \end{matrix} \right\}\right)$$

$$= -dg^{\sigma\tau}\{\ \}\{\ \} + 2\left\{ \begin{matrix} \sigma\,\lambda \\ \alpha \end{matrix} \right\} d\left(g^{\sigma\tau} g^{\beta\lambda}\left[\begin{matrix} \tau\,\alpha \\ \lambda \end{matrix} \right]\right)$$

$$\text{Es ist überdies } \left\{ \begin{matrix} \sigma\,\beta \\ \alpha \end{matrix} \right\} = \left\{ \begin{matrix} \beta\,\sigma \\ \alpha \end{matrix} \right\} \ \cdots (\alpha)$$

Mit Rücksicht darauf, dass sich das zweite Glied nicht ändert, wenn man die Summ. Indizes σ u β und gleichzeitig λ und τ vertauscht, ist das zweite Glied auch gleich

$$\left\{ \begin{matrix} \sigma\,\beta \\ \alpha \end{matrix} \right\} d\left(g^{\sigma\tau} g^{\beta\lambda}\left(\left[\begin{matrix} \tau\,\alpha \\ \lambda \end{matrix} \right] + \left[\begin{matrix} \lambda\,\alpha \\ \tau \end{matrix} \right]\right)\right)$$

oder gleich $\qquad \left\{ \begin{matrix} \sigma\,\beta \\ \alpha \end{matrix} \right\} d\left(g^{\sigma\tau} g^{\beta\lambda} \dfrac{\partial g_{\lambda\tau}}{\partial x_\alpha}\right)$

oder gleich $\qquad -\left\{ \begin{matrix} \sigma\,\beta \\ \alpha \end{matrix} \right\} dg^{\sigma\tau}_\alpha$

$$\text{Aus } g_{\varrho\sigma} g^{\sigma\tau} = \delta^\tau_\varrho \ \text{folgt nämlich}$$

$$\frac{\partial g_{\varrho\sigma}}{\partial x_\alpha} g^{\sigma\tau} = -g_{\varrho\sigma}\frac{\partial g^{\sigma\tau}}{\partial x_\alpha} \quad (\beta)$$

u. hieraus durch Multiplikation mit $g^{\varrho\lambda}$

$$g^{\varrho\lambda} g^{\sigma\tau}\frac{\partial g_{\varrho\sigma}}{\partial x_\alpha} = -\frac{\partial g^{\lambda\tau}}{\partial x_\alpha}$$

analog auch

$$g_{\varrho\lambda} g_{\sigma\tau}\frac{\partial g^{\varrho\sigma}}{\partial x_\alpha} = -\frac{\partial g_{\lambda\tau}}{\partial x_\alpha} \quad \left.\begin{matrix}\\\\\end{matrix}\right\}(\beta')$$

Es folgt also

$$dL = -\left\{ \begin{matrix} \sigma\,\beta \\ \alpha \end{matrix} \right\}\left\{ \begin{matrix} \tau\,\alpha \\ \beta \end{matrix} \right\} dg^{\sigma\tau} - \left\{ \begin{matrix} \sigma\,\beta \\ \alpha \end{matrix} \right\} dg^{\sigma\tau}_\alpha ,$$

woraus die Behauptung (1) folgt. Hieraus folgt, dass man die Gravitationsgleichungen in der Form

$$\frac{\partial}{\partial x_\alpha}\left(\frac{\partial L}{\partial g^{\sigma\tau}_\alpha}\right) - \frac{\partial L}{\partial g^{\sigma\tau}} = -\kappa\left(T_{\sigma\tau} - \tfrac{1}{2} g_{\sigma\tau} T\right) \ \cdots (2)$$

schreiben kann.

2) Erhaltungssätze.

Multipliziert man (2) mit $g^{\sigma\tau}_\beta$, so erhält man nach partieller Umformung z. Differentiation des ersten Gliedes

$$\frac{\partial}{\partial x_\alpha}\left(g^{\sigma\tau}_\beta \frac{\partial L}{\partial g^{\sigma\tau}_\alpha}\right) - \underbrace{\left(\frac{\partial L}{\partial g^{\sigma\tau}} g^{\sigma\tau}_\beta + \frac{\partial L}{\partial g^{\sigma\tau}_\alpha}\frac{\partial g^{\sigma\tau}_\alpha}{\partial x_\beta}\right)}_{\frac{\partial L}{\partial x_\beta}} = -\kappa\, T_{\sigma\tau}\, g^{\sigma\tau}_\beta$$

wegen Vertauschbarkeit von α und β

Das zweite Glied der rechten Seite verschwindet, wegen

$$g_{\sigma\tau}\frac{\partial g^{\sigma\tau}}{\partial x_\beta} = -g^{\sigma\tau}\frac{\partial g_{\sigma\tau}}{\partial x_\beta}$$

$$= -\frac{\partial \lg g}{\partial x_\beta} = 0$$

Nun schreibe ich den Erhaltungssatz für die Materie, indem ich ihn formal einführe, ohne seine Gültigkeit vorauszusetzen

$$\frac{\partial T_\mu^\sigma}{\partial x_\sigma} + \frac{1}{2} g_\mu^{\alpha\tau} T_{\alpha\tau} = A_\mu \quad \ldots\ldots (3)$$

(A_μ: unbekannte Raumfunktionen)

Das zweite Glied der linken Seite kann wegen (β) in die Form

$$-\frac{1}{2} \frac{\partial g_{\alpha\tau}}{\partial x_\mu} T^{\alpha\tau}$$

gebracht werden. Hierin lässt ich die { } einführen, was ich aber [illegible] brauchte.

Mit Hilfe davon lässt sich die rechte Seite der letzten Gleichung durch

$$2\kappa \frac{\partial T_\beta^\alpha}{\ldots} - 2\kappa A_\beta$$

ersetzen

$$A_\beta^\alpha - \frac{1}{2}\delta_\beta^\alpha A = -\frac{1}{\kappa} g^{\sigma\varepsilon} \left\{ {\sigma\tau \atop \alpha} \right\} \left\{ {\varepsilon\beta \atop \tau} \right\} \quad \ldots (7)$$

Abgesehen vom Faktor $-\frac{1}{\kappa}$ und der Bezeichnung der Indices stimmt die rechte Seite von (7) mit dem zweiten Glied in (6) überein, sodass man schreiben kann

$$\frac{\partial}{\partial x_\alpha}\left(g^{\tau\nu} \left\{ {\sigma\tau \atop \alpha} \right\} \right) = \kappa \left((T_\sigma^\nu + t_\sigma^\nu) - \frac{1}{2}\delta_\sigma^\nu (T + t) \right) \quad \ldots (8)$$

Diese Gleichung ist interessant, weil sie zeigt, dass das Entspringen der Gravitationslinien allein durch die Summe $T_\sigma^\nu + t_\sigma^\nu$ bestimmt ist, wie man ja auch erwarten muss.

ALBERT EINSTEIN

Born: March 14, 1879, in Ulm   Died: April 18, 1955, in Pasadena, California

"HE FORCED HIS SCIENTIFIC CONTEMPORARIES TO QUES-
TION AND REINTERPRET SUCH FUNDAMENTAL CATEGORIES
AS SPACE AND TIME. LATER, TO BE SURE, HE SUFFERED THE
FATE OF MANY OTHER REVOLUTIONARIES, WHO BOLDLY
TAKE THE FIRST STEPS ON A NEW ROAD BUT SHRINK FROM
THE NEXT STEPS. OTHERS MUST COME ALONG TO PICK UP
THE JOURNEY, BECAUSE THE ROAD SEEMS TOO SINISTER
TO ITS DISCOVERER. BUT EINSTEIN WAS THE FIRST TO SET
OUT WITH FULL DELIBERATION ON THE NEW PATHWAYS
OF SCIENCE."

Nobel Prize Winner Werner Heisenberg on Albert Einstein

Previous page: Albert Einstein.
Photo by Philippe Halsman, New York.

The text is a letter of Einstein to the Austrian
physicist, Paul Ehrenfest.

Right: In his special theory of relativity, Einstein
was led to an important equation: energy (E) is a
product of mass (M) and the square of the velocity
of light (c^2). It follows from this that even a very
small mass can be involved in a powerful energy
discharge. Among other things this equation describes
the energy-producing process within the sun, and so is
responsible for the existence of life. It also describes
the release of energy in a death-dealing nuclear
bomb. The blue light is the Cerenkov effect in a
nuclear reactor; it occurs when particles are
accelerated in a medium to velocities greater than that
of light in the same medium.

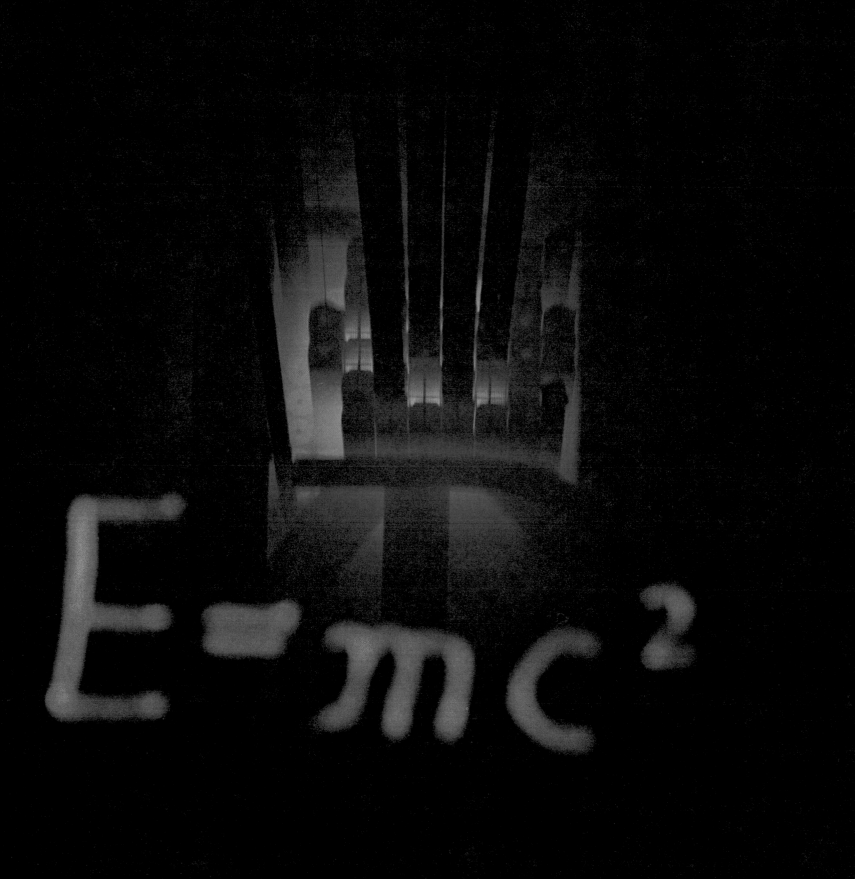

Left: In this laboratory at the Zurich
Federal Institute of Technology, Einstein
carried out his first experiments.

Right: Einstein rented this room in
Berne while he was working as a clerk
in the Swiss Patent Office. Here he wrote
up his theory of relativity.

Next page: the problem of simultaneity
and time in general plays a central role in
Einstein's theory of relativity. Einstein
put it this way: "There are only local
times. On earth, for example, everyone is
catapulted through space at the same
velocity — the velocity of the earth.
Thus all the clocks on earth run on
equally, and record 'earth' time. For a
body in motion like the earth, this is its
own time. . . . Now when two events take
place far away from each other spatially,
enormous periods of time are involved.
It is no longer possible to say which event
took place first and which second.
Depending on the velocity of the observer
vis-à-vis the event, either answer might
be made; and either would be true for a
given case."

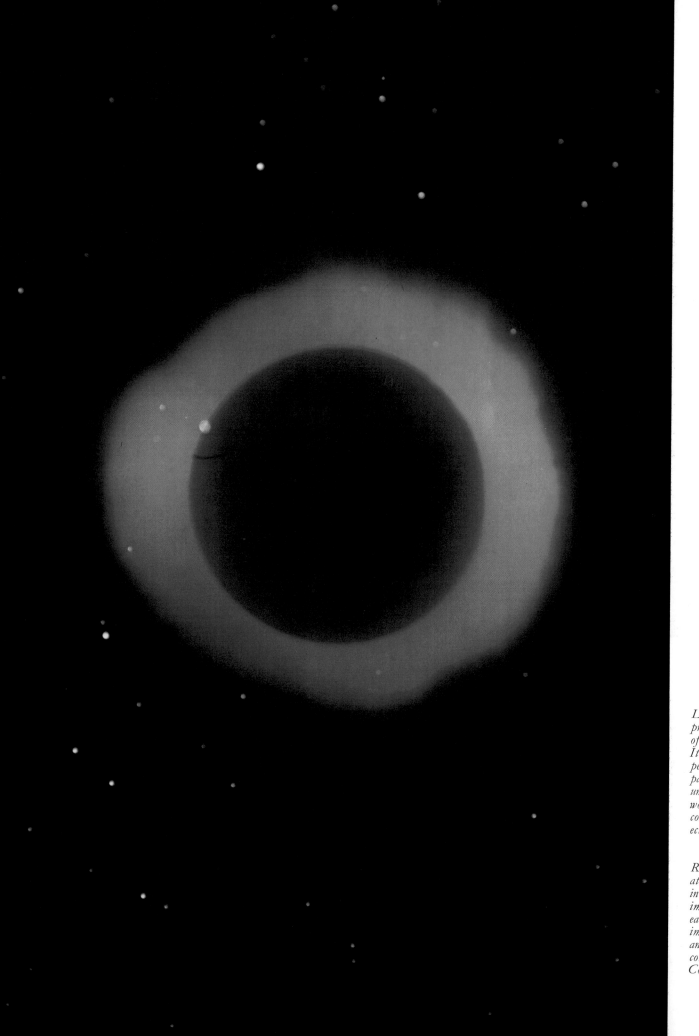

Left: The sun and the solar system provided Einstein with the first possibility of checking his theory of relativity. It predicted the precession of Mercury's perihelion and the bending of light rays passing near the sun. Expeditions were undertaken by solar physicists all over the world to check these phenomena, which could only be observed during a total eclipse of the sun (picture).

Right: Plexiglass model of uranium 235 atom, in which the nuclear molecules move in twisted paths. Uranium 235 plays an important role in nuclear physics. It is easy to split with thermal neutrons, so it is important in building nuclear reactors and nuclear bombs. This model was commissioned by the Union Carbide Corporation.

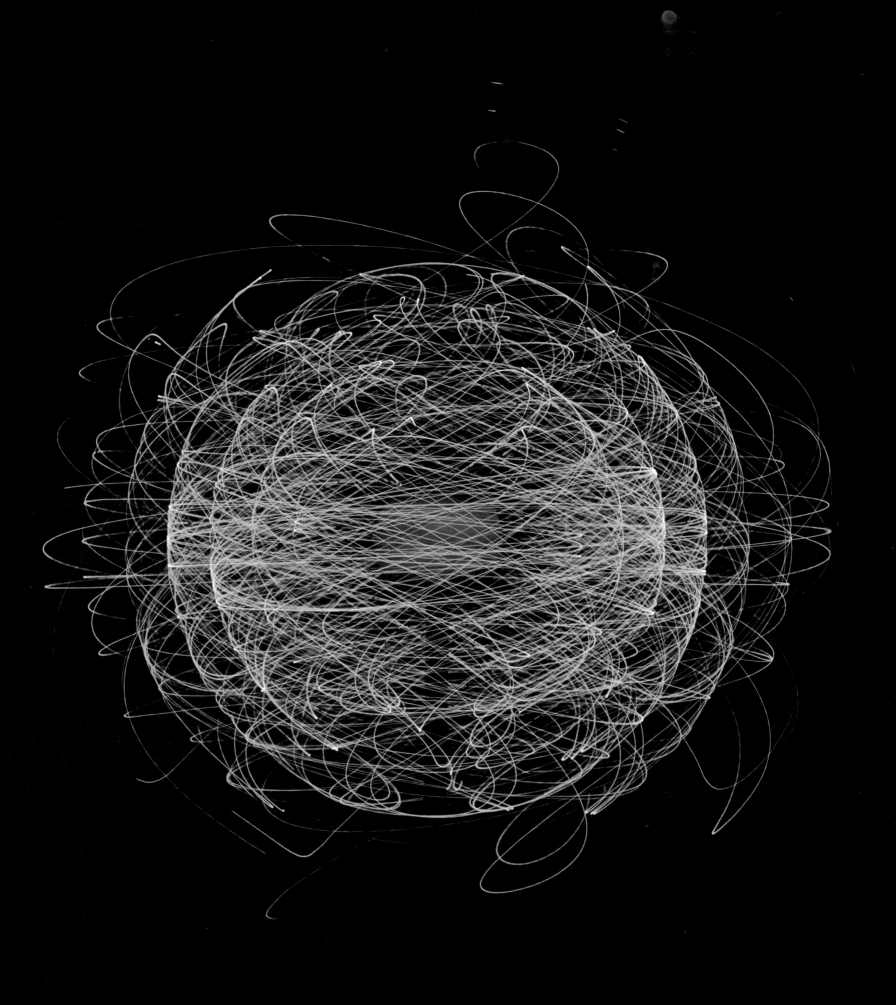

Below: There have been two major developments in recent physics. One is the Mössbauer effect, named after its discoverer, Rudolf L. Mössbauer. Radioactive nuclei are anchored in a crystal lattice in such a way that, on emitting gamma rays, they absorb no recoil energy. The rays thus acquire a precisely defined frequency and energy. This implies the possibility of astonishingly accurate time measurements, and it has stimulated attempts to test the theory of relativity. The other important development is the laser, a beam of light that is extremely coherent and defined. In physics it could be used to investigate the interaction of light and matter.

Right: Einstein's house at Princeton. Here he spent his years after his arrival in America. He lectured at the University and worked on his general field theory. Death came before he could finish it.

THE SYMBOL OF AN EPOCH

The place of Einstein in modern physics was well described by Werner Heisenberg: "Wherever people talk about science and technology, wherever comments or complaints are made about its abstruseness and its isolation from everyday realities, Albert Einstein seems to be the living symbol of this whole field—just as Picasso seems to symbolize modern art."

For most people the theories of Einstein are no more comprehensible than the cosmologies of old. His symbols and equations seem just as mysterious as the superstitions of the ancient world. Einstein is the genius who dominated an age, who redefined the physical relationship between space, time, and the velocity of light. He toppled the prevailing view of the universe, and the atom bomb is not the only explosive force that resulted from his work. He unleashed ideas that have not yet spent their force. Man's conception of finiteness and infinity has been altered, and time and space have been quantified in Einstein's abstruse equations.

The layman, of course, can no longer follow the full train of thought. Newton's celestial mechanics were complicated, but with some effort a person could make sense out of them. By contrast, the theories of modern physics and astrophysics are clouded in mystery. When one attempts to explain these mathematical theories in words, misunderstanding and confusion result. That is why Albert Einstein seems to represent the new mythology of modern man.

70. Max Planck, *winner of the Nobel Prize in physics in 1918. In 1900 he discovered that radiated energy is not divisible at will, that it shows up as small individual units—each called a "quantum." The resultant "quantum theory" is a discontinuity theory, while Einstein's theory of relativity is a continuity theory.* $E = mc^2$ *characterizes Einstein's formula for the relationship between mass and energy. Planck's formula is* $E = h \cdot v$: *the radiated energy (E) is a product of its frequency (v) and the Planckian action quantum (h).*

TEAMWORK IN MODERN SCIENCE

Even an Einstein could not have worked out his theories if it had not been for the many advances made by science before his day. New developments in logic and mathematics had their impact on physics. We shall mention a few points that show clearly how the various scientific disciplines interacted.

In the nineteenth century, James C. Maxwell (1831–1879) developed a revolutionary theory about electricity and magnetism. It stressed the mutual interaction of electric and magnetic fields, and proposed an electromagnetic theory of light waves. The "wave" theory of light seemed to have superseded the "corpuscular" theory. Then, in 1887, Heinrich Hertz (1857–1894) discovered the laws of the photoelectric effect, which could not be explained by Maxwell's theory.

Soon after, around 1900, Max Planck (1858–1947) formulated his famous quantum theory, introducing the notion of two basic elements, the elementary quantum and the action quantum. On the basis of this theory, Einstein worked out a new theory of light. Underlying it was the notion that there were basic light quanta, which Ein-

EINSTEIN: THE THEORY OF RELATIVITY

Two important experiments served as the background for Einstein's theoretical contributions to physics. In 1887 Michelson and Morley attempted to measure the velocity of the earth through the aether; the results inspired Einstein to formulate his special theory of relativity in 1905. In 1915, L. Eötvös conducted experiments on the relationship between weight and inertia; the conclusions inspired Einstein to formulate his general theory of relativity in 1915.

THE MICHELSON-MORLEY EXPERIMENTS

Michelson and Morley wanted to measure the effect of the earth's motion on the velocity of light. One measurement was taken with the sunlight striking the earth's orbit at a right angle; the expected result was 186,000 miles per second, and this was verified. Another measurement was taken at such an angle that the velocity of earth itself (18.2 miles per second) would be added to the velocity of light. The unexpected and inexplicable result was 186,000 miles per second. No matter how they tried, they could not get the velocity of the earth into their final calculations. Why?

In pre-Copernican days the answer would have been simple enough: the earth does not move. But classical Newtonian physics could not explain why the resultant figure was not the sum of the two velocities at work. Einstein began with the assumption that Michelson's results had to be taken seriously. Since no other velocity apparently could be added to the velocity of light, the latter velocity must be the highest velocity anywhere. In short, Einstein did not contradict classical physics, he merely reformulated its operation at the upper end of the scale; his work deals with relationships near the velocity of light, both in the cosmos and in the realm of the atom (since light originates in atomic processes).

Now if we accept the velocity of light as an upper limit, important consequences follow. At such velocities, the concept of "simultaneity" loses its accustomed meaning. It now depends on spatial factors or, as the physicists put it, on the frame of reference in which the observations take place. Moreover, time can no longer be regarded as an absolute. Processes take place faster or slower depending on whether they are propelled slower or faster; thus bodies that are propelled extremely rapidly suffer a diminution in length.

One of the most noteworthy and momentous consequences of Einstein's theory, provable only with a complicated mathematical apparatus, is that matter and energy are equivalent. To put it another way, matter is merely one particular configuration of energy. We should be able to make matter disappear and have energy appear in its place. The special theory of relativity even provided the applicable mathematical formula, $E = mc^2$: energy is the product of mass and the square of the velocity of light. Knowing the background behind this theory, we should not be surprised to find the velocity of light in the equation.

Einstein's equation provided one of the touchstones for nuclear physics. Astrophysicists were quick to realize that they might now be able to probe the sources of stellar energy. By 1934 they knew that stellar energy resulted from nuclear reactions in the interior of the stars. Suppose, for example, that four hydrogen atoms were added to form a helium atom; the result would be a mass deficiency which would show up as a huge radiation of energy. The detonation of the hydrogen bomb proves that this is no phantom hypothesis; its release of energy is based on the same principle. The reverse process is also feasible in the laboratory; scientists can convert huge amounts of energy into particles of matter.

Einstein's special theory of relativity radically transformed our notion of time. Physics could no longer hold on to "absolute time." And Newton's "absolute space" fared no better in Einstein's theories.

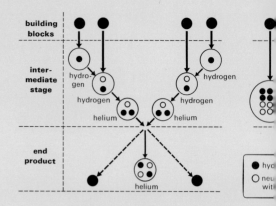

The two ways in which a helium atom can be derived from 4 hydrogen atoms in the interior of the stars. On the left: first heavy hydrogen, then light helium, then normal helium. Right: a normal carbon atom takes on 4 hydrogen atoms, turns into heavy carbon, nitrogen, and oxygen atoms, and then into helium.

THE EXPERIMENTS OF EÖTVÖS

Classical physics attributed two basic characteristics to mass: weight and inertia. In everyday language we would say that a body was heavy, and that it tended to resist any attempt to set it in motion.

In a series of careful experiments, the Hungarian physicist L. Eötvös (1848–1919) argued that the inertial mass was proportional to the gravitational mass. Einstein decided to carry this idea further. He asserted that the two masses were in fact identical, that they were merely two different aspects of the same physical quality. The mathematical formulation of this hypothesis was extremely difficult, but Einstein wisely incorporated the mathematical ideas of B. Riemann (1826–1866) and H. Minkowski (1864–1909) on non-Euclidean, four-dimensional geometry. The result was a picture devoid of all clarity, a theory of "closed, hyperspherical, positively curved space." We shall return to this notion later.

What interests us here is how the general theory of relativity deals with the force of gravitation, which played such an important role in Newton's theory of planetary motion. In effect, Einstein explained planetary motion without invoking the mysterious concept of gravitation at all. The nature of this force had remained a mystery since Newton's day, despite any and all attempts to explain its nature.

According to Einstein's general theory of relativity, the orbit of a planet results from the fact that the huge mass of the sun "curves" the surrounding space; the curved orbit is actually the shortest orbit for the planet. Thus the "attracted" planet takes a curved orbit because the surrounding space is actually curved by virtue of

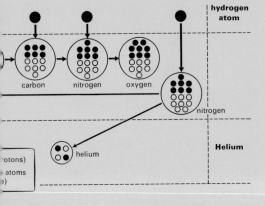

hydrogen
atom

carbon   nitrogen   oxygen

nitrogen

Helium

the existing mass. In other words, gravitation is a characteristic of space itself, not some independent entity.

Now at first glance Einstein's theory may seem to be merely more elegant than Newton's. In fact, it may not look as good because of its complicated mathematical apparatus and its lack of clarity. But Einstein himself proved that his theory was not simply an exercise in elegance and obfuscation. He made three predictions which were subject to experimental verification; and they dealt with astronomy, a field which had not been directly involved at all in the formulation of the theory.

EINSTEIN'S THREE PREDICTIONS

One general observation must be kept in mind with regard to both the special and the general theory of relativity. So long as we are dealing with earthly dimensions and magnitudes, Newtonian physics will prove fully satisfactory; but when we start to deal with enormous masses or with velocities approaching the speed of light, we must shift to the more comprehensive theory of relativity. Newtonian physics, then, is a special instance under the theory of relativity.

In formulating his theories, Einstein predicted that three things could be verified by astronomical observation and easily explained if his theories were correct. What were these three things? Have they been verified?

1. The precession of Mercury's perihelion. The perihelion of a planet is that point in its orbit when it is nearest to the sun. It exists because the planet's orbit is not a circle but an ellipse, whose focal point is the sun. When we talk about the precession of a planet's perihelion, we mean that the planet's orbit slowly meanders around the sun in a rosette-shaped path; it does not remain fixed in one position.

Precession of a planet's perihelion. Perihel at start (P₁), and after a certain length of time (P₂), say 100 years. The arrow shows the direction of the planet's rotation and the precession of the perihelion.

On the basis of his formulations, Einstein attempted to work out the motion of Mercury's perihelion. Here the phenomenon was most pronounced because of Mercury's extremely eccentric orbit. Einstein's result was the exact figure, 43 seconds of arc per century, which still puzzled classical physics. The first proof had turned out successfully.

2. Light deflection by a gravitational field. Picture a light ray coming towards earth from some distant star and passing near the sun. According to the general theory of relativity, it must pass through a sharply curved portion of space near the sun; as a result, this light ray will be deflected. So said Einstein in 1915.

This phenomenon should be observable during a total eclipse of the sun. If a reading is taken of the relevant area during a total eclipse, then compared with a night reading of the same area a half year earlier, we should find that the stars in the immediate vicinity of the sun should show a shift of 1.75 seconds of arc. Astronomers have spent much time, effort, and money in trying to verify this effect. It certainly seems to be in the proper order of magnitude; but errors in astronomical calculation, which would have to be compensated for, have complicated the process of interpretation. Today scientists play down this proof, all the more because a third proof has been verified fully in laboratories on earth.

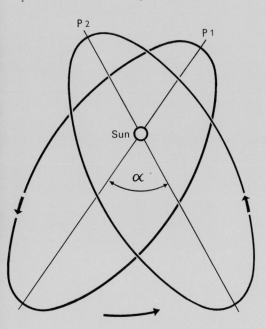

P 2

P 1

Sun

α

3. Frequency shift in a gravitational field. As early as 1911 Einstein offered a third possibility for verifying his theory. On the basis of his theory, he asserted that light coming from a celestial body with a large gravitational field should show a red shift in its spectral lines. This was so because a strong gravitational field slows down the time cycle which would normally take place. The result should then show up as a red shift in the spectral lines.

Here, too, the astrophysicists expended much effort trying to verify this effect. Once again, however, they had to put up with many sources of interference; by 1960 they had become quite sceptical about the chances for verifying Einstein's assertion. But with the aid of the *Mössbauer effect,* Einstein's hypothesis became accessible to verification in the laboratory.

Rudolf Mössbauer (1929) discovered the possibility of emitting gamma rays (having extremely short wave lengths) in such a way that they acquire a precisely defined frequency and energy. Scientists developed the technique for measuring the frequency shift of a Mössbauer line with a gamma ray source under free fall in the laboratory. Thus the Einstein prediction of a red shift in the spectral lines from a body with a large gravitational field can be tested in the earth's gravitational field. This was done in 1960 and the result confirmed Einstein's prediction to within $\pm 10\%$.

In general we can say that today no physicist would question the special theory of relativity, and that only a few physicists challenge the basic conclusions of the general theory of relativity. The latter do so because many important questions have not yet been solved to everyone's satisfaction. But it seems that the general theory of relativity can prove fruitful for astronomy in the future, specifically with regard to the nature of quasars.

Quasars appear to be starlike objects, but they also send out very strong radio signals. Astronomers are not sure how to interpret the marked red shift in the spectral lines of quasars. The red shift could be the *Doppler effect* (see page 23*), in which case quasars would be enormously distant from us. But it could also be the result of a frequency shift in a gravitational field, in which case quasars could be relatively close to us. There are theoretical complications with either interpretation. Up to now the classical theories have not provided a satisfactory explanation. Further work on the general theory of relativity could provide the only feasible approach to the solution of the border-line case. Finally, Einstein's theory of relativity has provided astronomy with new ideas on space and time; as a result, cosmology has been able to work out new models of the overall structure of the universe.

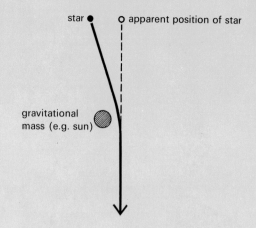

The schematic diagram of light deflection in the proximity of a large mass, for example the sun.

71. *Lord Ernest Rutherford (1871–1937). One of the big three in modern physics. Unlike Planck and Einstein, he was of a practical bent. He showed experimentally that the atom is built up around a nucleus, and that it is subject to enormous changes rather than being an immutable body. He is rightly called the father of nuclear physics.*

stein called "photons." Despite this boost to the quantum theory, Einstein later adopted a critical attitude towards it. He did not want to take part in the further development of quantum physics, in which the concept of causality is more or less replaced by statistical predictions about large numbers of particles.

Einstein's scepticism about quantum physics lasted throughout his life; it persuaded him to attempt to formulate a "unified field theory," encompassing gravitation, electromagnetism, and subatomic phenomena under one set of laws. He wanted to shore up the rift which the quantum theory had introduced into physics. But he himself admitted that he could not provide a pure field theory that would also cover the atomic structure of matter.

Einstein was stimulated by the ideas of many other scientists, and his work was based on the foundation they provided. As he put it: "Every day I remind myself that my external and interior life is based on the work of other scientists, past and present. So I must make every effort to give something in return for all that I receive from others."

EINSTEIN THE MAN

Despite his genius for mathematics and physics, Albert Einstein was a man like anyone else. He himself made no claim to be anything else. He discouraged the cult of personality, and he was not an ivory-tower bookworm. The physics genius was also a passionate social democrat, fiercely maintaining that all men had the same basic rights. He was a staunch supporter of public education. He once wrote: "It will not do if results of science are known and developed merely by a small handful of experts. If scientific knowledge becomes the exclusive property of a small elite, the philosophical spirit of the nation's people will be weakened and debilitated."

Einstein was a simple, unassuming man. There was not a trace of arrogance in his makeup. In fact, he was rather shy. He enjoyed his leisure, delighting in good food and his pipe. He loved nature, and often played the violin. Like many people he enjoyed sport and especially sailing. And he thoroughly enjoyed Charlie Chaplin films. He was a sturdy man of medium size and average health. He tended to wear shabby suits, and on one occasion he was asked to pay his hotel bill in advance. The famous scientist did not look the part. In his younger days he sometimes passed the time in some dark corner of a café, mulling over his ideas. He did not take himself too seriously. "There are often times when I don't think about anything at all," he once said. And he described his talent this way: "I'm not particularly gifted, but I have this insatiable curiosity."

Einstein was keenly interested in the political events of his time. He was always ready to offer his personal aid, and he did help many people. But he also took a public stand on social issues. He spoke out against fanatic nationalism and aggressive militarism. Though he was not a Marxist, Einstein supported the aims of the labor movement and sympathized with the programs of democratic socialism.

Einstein looked forward to the day when the masses would achieve real intellectual freedom through sound education. After returning from a trip to the East Indies, he was asked if he had used a rickshaw. His reply clearly indicated his own feeling on social questions: "I would never allow myself to be drawn by another human being, as if he were a beast of burden."

Einstein's family background and training explained his views to a large extent. He came from a Jewish family of German nationality. His Swabian dialect was a source of amusement to many, but it was not an affectation. His ancestors had lived in that region for a long time. Einstein never gave up the German tongue, using it in most of the lectures he gave around the world.

His father had also been gifted in mathematics, but he could not follow up his studies because his family was too poor. Nor were his own finances in great shape when Albert was born in Ulm on March 14, 1879. At the time his electrical workshop was not doing very well. A year after Albert's birth, the family went to Munich. There the father opened up another workshop, as a joint venture with his brother. They also built a small factory that manufactured lamps, dynamos, and measuring devices. Business went badly, and the factory had to be sold.

Albert was a quiet child, and he did not learn to talk easily. In grammar school he disliked physical education. But he found mathematics extremely easy. At twelve, he took up Euclid. Studying alone, he worked out his own solution to the Pythagorean theorem. He later described his private progress during this period thus: "Between twelve and sixteen I familiarized myself with the basic elements of mathematics, including the fundamentals of differential and integral calculus."

But school was difficult for him. He did not like learning by rote, and he opposed instruction in fencing. Imbued with his family's spirit of intellectual freedom, he had no liking for the authoritarianism of the German school system. One teacher advised him to leave the school, claiming that his presence in the class was enough to destroy respect for authority. Other teachers, however, recognized his talent and tried to develop it.

When Albert was fifteen, his father went bankrupt and had to wind up his business. The family headed for Milan, but Albert was supposed to stay in Munich to finish school. A few weeks later, however, Albert followed his family to Milan. For several weeks he attended the International School in Milan, which was run by a Swiss educator who followed the methods of Pestalozzi. Here Albert had difficulty with foreign languages.

Finally, the father sent him to a trade school in the Swiss town of Aarau. Albert was happy with school for the first time. The headmaster treated him as one of his own children, and took him into his own home. There Albert made friends with the headmaster's seven children. One of the headmaster's sons later married Albert's sister, Maja.

At the age of seventeen, Albert entered the Federal Institute of Technology in Zurich, one of the best colleges of its kind in Europe. He led the life of a poor student, living in cheap lodgings, tutoring, and going without meals. From the autumn of 1896 to summer 1900, he majored in mathematics, geometry and physics; but he also

72. Letter of Einstein in which he voices his stand on the 1948 Arab-Israeli War and the two great power blocks.

took courses in the humanities and in social studies. Einstein later admitted that he had been somewhat remiss in his study of mathematics, even though his teachers had been excellent. He was fascinated with the direct contact involved in experimentation, and he spent most of his time in the physics lab. His interest in scientific experimentation was greater than his interest in mathematics. Only later did he come to perceive the close connexion between "the basic tenets of physics and refined mathematical methodology."

The young genius did not have an easy time in the Institute either. Here, too, he had differences with his professors. One teacher remarked: "You are an intelligent young man, Einstein, but you have one big fault. You won't listen to anyone." The problem was that Einstein refused to do an assignment as prescribed. He insisted on working out a solution in his own way.

When he finished his final exams, Einstein entered the most difficult period of his life. His family could not support him any longer. When the opportunity presented itself, he would take odd jobs related to scientific work. At one point he was involved in some research work on sunspots. He then became a supply teacher at a technical school in Winterthur, replacing a professor who had been called into the army. His income was small, and it was during this period that he apparently contracted a chronic stomach ailment; he also became a Swiss citizen. From his meager monthly income, he set aside a small amount to pay for the costs involved in becoming a Swiss citizen.

A REVOLUTIONARY CIVIL SERVANT

In 1902 decisive changes took place in Einstein's life. At twenty-three he was now wholly on his own. He was not satisfied with the varying fortunes of a supply teacher. A friend's father recommended him for a post in the Swiss Patent Office in Berne. Einstein got the job, and was hired as a technical expert—third class. Now his steady but small yearly income allowed him to get an apartment and to get married.

He had been in love with another student at the Institute of Technology, Mileva Maritsch, since his first year there. She was a Serbian, whose parents were of Hungarian stock. Their common interest in mathematics and physics brought them together. Even at that time they had announced their engagement. Mileva finished her studies a year after Einstein, with help from him. She followed him to Berne, where they were married quietly.

Einstein's parents did not particularly care for their would-be daughter-in-law. She seemed strange to them, and she suffered from tuberculosis. She had no taste for housework, and took little care of her appearance. But she was a real intellectual companion to the young scientist, sharing his work and supporting him in his way of doing things.

Einstein's job in the Patent Office was relatively easy for him. Basically, he had to

155

prepare patent documents, making sure that the claims for an invention were formulated clearly and correctly. Though he had to spend eight hours a day at his desk, Einstein liked the job because he had a lot of time to work on his own theories.

For his own work Einstein needed only a few things: books, paper, pens, and time. It was not experimental work that required laboratory facilities. Books were his basic tools. All his new ideas were based on data that had been obtained experimentally by others.

In 1901 Einstein published his first research work in the *Annalen der Physik*. A second investigation was published in 1902. Three years later there appeared the five papers that brought him world renown. He submitted the first to the University of Zurich, and received a doctorate for it. The second brought him the 1921 Nobel Prize in physics. But the most famous of these five papers was the fourth, which contained the special theory of relativity; it was rejected as a doctoral thesis by the University of Zurich. These five papers created a sensation in the scholarly world. Some reacted violently against them, feeling that they abrogated all the old conceptual categories. Others applauded them loudly.

Einstein never regarded himself as a revolutionary in physics. He himself had this to say about the theory of relativity: "The theory of relativity is hardly a revolutionary theory. It was a natural development along the line that science had been following for centuries. To be sure, one cannot arbitrarily decide to refashion such seemingly fundamental categories as space, time, and motion. It must be done on the basis of factual observation. The general theory owes its origin to the observed numerical equivalence of inertial and gravitational mass in bodies—a fundamental fact for which classical mechanics could not provide any interpretation." But today there is general agreement that Einstein forced his contemporaries to re-examine all these basic concepts.

In the summer of 1905, Einstein was invited for the first time to lecture on his theory. The invitation was to conduct a seminar for theoretical physics at the University of Berne. But Einstein did not want to leave his job in the Patent Office. He was afraid that the preparation of lectures would take up too much time; moreover, his income as a lecturer would not match his existing salary, and he now had a family to support.

Einstein's first child had just been born. The new father worked intensively. His only source of relaxation was music. For many years he played second violin in a string quartet, along with a lawyer, a bookbinder, a mathematics teacher, and a prison warden. The group preferred works by Haydn, Mozart, and Beethoven.

Finally, in 1907, he gave in to insistent pleas and decided to set out on an academic career. After some hesitation he gave his first lectures in Berne in the winter of 1908–1909. He had an audience of four students. By the summer of 1909, only one student remained. Einstein found it difficult at first not to talk over the heads of his audience. Even professors found his theory too abstruse.

That year, however, he was appointed to the post of extraordinary professor at the University of Zurich. His old friend from student days, Friedrich Adler, was largely responsible for this appointment. The board of trustees favored Adler for the

73. Letter of Einstein to his mother, informing her that observations by others during solar eclipses have verified his theory about stellar light deflection around the sun's periphery.

appointment, but he declined. He said: "If we can get a man like Einstein, it would be foolish not to appoint him. I must say, quite candidly, that my ability as a research physicist is far below Einstein's."

THE PROOF OF THE THEORY OF RELATIVITY

Einstein was on the road to success. On December 11, 1909, he gave his inaugural lecture on "The Role of Atomic Theory in the Current Physics." He now took great pains to make his lectures comprehensible to the students. He repeatedly asked whether they could follow his line of thought, abandoned all fancy rhetoric, and injected humor whenever he could. Soon he had established real contact with his audience, and the students flocked around him to ask questions during the breaks. He seldom spoke from a prepared manuscript, preferring to develop his thoughts from notes that he had jotted down. He would often continue the dialogue with them in some café, and then, after closing-time, invite them back to his house for coffee.

Invitations to lecture poured in from universities all over Europe. He was offered a permanent post by many renowned universities from Leiden to Prague. Madame Curie, the discoverer of radium, made a special effort to get him to Prague.

In the autumn of 1910, Kaiser Franz Josef I appointed him extraordinary professor at the German University in Prague. Einstein's scientific renown had won over anti-Jewish prejudice. But Einstein did not feel at home there. He had the facilities of a large institute at his disposal and could carry on his work as he pleased; but he did not like the mood of antisemitism that pervaded the city. While he was in Prague. he received more invitations—from Vienna, New York, and Utrecht. Various universities offered him permanent posts. When Einstein received an offer from his alma mater, the Federal Institute of Technology in Zurich, he could not refuse it. He resigned the imperial professorship, and returned to Zurich in the summer of 1912.

Einstein found many scientists to collaborate with him. Old and new friends stood by him, discussing his problems with him, offering corrections, and the stimulation of their ideas. In Zurich Einstein again established ties with an old school friend, Marcel Grossmann. On the basis of preliminary work done by others, they jointly worked out an "outline of a general theory of relativity and a theory of gravitation" (1913), of which Einstein provided a definitive statement in 1916.

Once again offers poured in to Einstein from various universities. Max Planck, the creator of the quantum theory, arrived in Zurich to persuade Einstein to go to Berlin. After thinking it over, Einstein accepted the offer. In November 1913 he was made a regular member of the Berlin Academy of Science, taking his place in the physics and mathematics section.

He arrived in Berlin at a bad time. He had scarcely settled down when World War I broke out. During the war little attention was paid to Einstein and his scientific theories. But things changed radically when peace came. Now the astronomers would have opportunities to prove or disprove his theory.

Einstein himself had remarked that the bending of light rays, predicted by his theory of relativity, could be measured during a solar eclipse. As a matter of fact, in 1914 a German expedition had set out for Siberia to observe a solar eclipse there. But when war broke out, the members of the expedition were arrested and then deported. Now, in May 1919, solar eclipses were visible in Brazil and North Africa.

The Royal Society organized two expeditions to observe these eclipses. They returned with enough data to prove that Einstein's theory was correct. He had predicted that during a solar eclipse the stars in the vicinity of the sun would appear to shift their position by 1.75 seconds of arc relative to their position when the sun was not in that part of the sky. The photographs of the eclipse attested this phenomenon. This proved that the light rays coming from these stars had been deflected by the sun's gravitational field. Scientists hastened to inform Einstein and to congratulate him. His reply was: "I need no proof; save it for others who do."

Now Einstein's name was on everybody's lips. All over the world books and articles about him appeared. Even the general populace seemed to grasp something of the significance of his theory. He was besieged by reporters, photographers, and autograph hunters. Hollywood wanted to make a film about him, and he was offered a handsome fee. Einstein's only comment was: "The world has gone mad."

In 1919 Einstein's marriage with Mileva was dissolved. His wife had not liked the idea of moving to Prague, and she later refused to follow him to Berlin. The separation eventually led to a divorce. Einstein still showed an interest in his family; he was concerned about his son's education, and he gave his first wife the 50,000 dollars that came with the Nobel prize.

His second wife was his cousin, Elsa Einstein. She had been left a widow early in life, and she had two little girls. When Einstein came to Berlin, he renewed their childhood friendship. They were married in 1919, and they lived happily together until Elsa's death in 1936. Elsa did not know anything about physics and mathematics; but she did know how to create a good atmosphere in the home, and how to provide the quiet environment Albert needed for his work. She acted as his secretary, and was an ideal companion.

Einstein was one of the first Germans to be invited abroad after World War I. After giving lectures in the United States, he was invited to London in June 1921. His host, Lord Haldane, gave a dinner in his honor; among the invited guests were the Archbishop of Canterbury and the President of the Royal Astronomical Society, Professor Eddington. The Prime Minister declined the invitation, sending a personal letter of apology for his absence.

There was still strong anti-German sentiment in Britain because of the air raids during the war. When Einstein entered the auditorium of King's College to deliver his lecture, he met with an icy reception. There was even some fear that a riot would occur when Einstein began to lecture in German. Lord Haldane introduced his guest as the Newton of the twentieth century, not mentioning that he was a German and a Jew. Einstein began his lecture with a brief eulogy of Newton before going

74. Letter of Einstein reporting his communiqué to President Roosevelt about the possibility of manufacturing an atomic bomb.

158

on to explain his theory of relativity. He electrified the audience, and won them over completely. Singlehanded, he had re-established cultural ties between Germany and England.

THE REFUGEE

Though he was well liked, Einstein was persecuted like Galileo and forced to emigrate like Kepler. A wave of nationalism swept the defeated Germany, and with it came antisemitism. Einstein was both a pacifist and a Jew. He had refused to sign a manifesto by German scientists which exonerated Germany from all guilt for the war. Moreover, he had spoken out in favor of the Zionist movement, which sought to create a homeland for Jews in Israel.

Einstein was not a zealous Zionist or Jewish nationalist; he was a cosmopolitan. In 1925, along with Gandhi, Tagore, Wells, Barbusse, Unamuno, and others, he signed a manifesto opposing universal military service and championing personal freedom and world brotherhood.

The zealous German nationalists now came to regard him as their arch-enemy. His person and his theories became the butt of their hatred. It soon reached the point where it was not safe for Einstein to live in Germany. Threatening letters came in the mail, attacks on him appeared in the press, there was veiled talk of assassination.

In 1922 Einstein was invited to lecture in Japan. There, too, he spoke in German, remaining three months. On the return trip he visited Palestine, now a British protectorate, where a Jewish colony had taken root. A Jewish university was already under construction on Mount Olivet, and Einstein had raised most of the money for the project. In the half-finished building Einstein delivered the first lecture to be given there. From Palestine Einstein went to Spain, where he was received by King Alfonso XIII and inducted into the Academy of Science. The Minister of Education offered him a home in Spain, but Einstein declined.

Shortly after his return to Germany, there were new threats on his life. The same clique that had murdered Rathenau now focused their sights on him. His wife and friends persuaded him to accept an invitation from Holland and to remain there for a while. But soon he was back in Germany, and the threats continued.

Around this time Einstein's health took a serious turn. He had already suffered several physical breakdowns from overwork. Around the age of fifty, he began to have severe heart attacks. He now had to be very careful about his health. There would be no more long walks and no more pipe-smoking. Only after a long period of recuperation was he able to return to his work.

He spent the whole of the following year working on his unified field theory. On another trip to the United States in 1932, he was asked how much longer he would be working on the field theory. He replied: "I shall have the rest of my life to work on this problem."

On this trip he made the acquaintance of Dr. Abraham Flexner, the famous American educator. Flexner was anxious to reform the educational system in America, and he was the driving force behind the establishment of the Institute for

Advanced Study at Princeton. He found someone to put up five million dollars for the project. Only top-notch research scholars were to be selected as members. Flexner offered Einstein a life-time membership of the Institute. Einstein accepted on condition that he would have to spend only five months each year in the United States. He asked for such a small fee that Flexner increased it.

But then a stumbling block appeared. A patriotic woman's organization accused Einstein of Communism, and urged that he be refused an entry permit. Einstein decided to give up the whole idea. But so many influential people came to his support that his visa was granted in a short time. Luck was with him.

While Einstein was touring America, Hitler came to power in Germany. The persecution of the Jews began in earnest. When Einstein arrived back in Europe, he stopped for a time in Belgium. There he learned that Hitler had put a price on his head. In Belgium detectives had to protect him from would-be assassins. The dowager queen, with whom he played music each week, protected him as long as she could. Under great secrecy he traveled to England, and from there back to the United States. He was brought into the country secretly and lodged at Princeton. Meanwhile, in Germany, his home and possessions were being confiscated.

75. Otto Hahn (1879–1968). Together with L. Meitner and E. Strassmann, he conducted the first important experiments on splitting the atom with slow-speed neutrons.

A LETTER LEADS TO A BOMB

On August 2, 1939, exactly one month before war broke out in Europe, Einstein wrote a portentous letter to President Roosevelt:

> Recent experiments by E. Fermi and L. Szilard, which I have seen in manuscript, justify the belief that in the near future uranium can be developed into a new and significant source of energy. Certain aspects of the whole situation call for special attention and, if necessary, quick action on the part of the government. . . .

76. Lise Meitner (*1878). Participating in Hahn's atom-splitting experiments, she interpreted the result as a fission of the uranium nucleus and deduced that vast amounts of energy had been liberated.

> In the course of the last four months — thanks to the work of Joliot in France, and Fermi and Szilard in America — it has become apparent that a chain reaction can be set off in a large mass of uranium, releasing considerable energy and a huge quantity of radium-like elements. . . .

> This new phenomenon could also lead to the construction of bombs. It is conceivable, though by no means certain, that extraordinarily powerful bombs of a totally new type could be built. A single bomb of this type, carried on a ship and exploded in a harbor, could well demolish the whole harbor and part of the surrounding area. . . .

> As I understand it, Germany has recently halted the sale of uranium from the Czech mines she has taken over. Her quick action in this area may be explained by the fact that the son of the Under-Secretary of State is now enrolled in the Kaiser Wilhelm Institute, where some of the American research on uranium is now being imitated.

This letter, which eventually led to the development of the atom bomb, followed

160

77. *Niels Bohr (1885–1962). He did some of the basic groundwork on atomic and quantum physics. His model of the atom's structure became basic to all physics. He was the first to draw the correct conclusions about Hahn's atom-splitting experiments and the energy gain involved.*

78. *Enrico Fermi (1901–1954). He worked with great success on nuclear chain reactions and isotope separation. He played a major role in the construction of the first nuclear reactor.*

upon the splitting of the atom in 1938 by a group of German physicists. Three atomic physicists — Otto Hahn, E. Strassmann, and Lise Meitner — had bombarded uranium atoms with neutrons; the result was a new element, which appeared to be even more radioactive than uranium itself. The group was not clearly aware that they had split the uranium atom; but Lise Meitner drew this conclusion and continued her research along these lines.

At this time the persecution of Jews was intensified in Germany. Lise Meitner, a brilliant scientist and a long-time assistant of Max Planck, was also a Jew. Only her reputation saved her from direct persecution. Pressure was exerted to force her to continue her atomic research in Germany. Fearing for her life and unwilling to help the German war machine, she managed to escape to Sweden. Although she could only take scattered memoranda with her, she was able to complete her research in Sweden. Soon after her arrival in that country, she published her theoretical interpretation of the atom-splitting experiment.

Her data reached Professor Niels Bohr at Columbia University. He and Professor Enrico Fermi repeated the experiment. At the University of Chicago Leo Szilard, who was in contact with Fermi and Bohr, was doing similar research work. He was the first to give a detailed report on the possibilities of an atomic war. When Szilard described the potential of atomic energy he said there was every reason to believe that if one could use higher speed neutrons, it would be easy to construct extremely dangerous bombs. The destructive force of such bombs could only be roughly estimated. But there was no doubt that they would far outstrip all military expectations.

The conclusion from all this was that America must hasten to build atomic bombs before some other power did. Einstein recognized this conclusion and the concomitant danger: "I was well aware of the fearful danger that the success of this undertaking might involve for mankind. But the probability that the Germans were working on the same project forced me to take this step."

Einstein himself merely recommended that the project be undertaken. He did not work directly on it, although some of his formulas in the theory of relativity did point to the utilization of nuclear energy. By establishing a calculable relationship between mass and energy, he showed how all the energy present in matter could be set free. Moreover, while Hitler's war machine ploughed over Europe, he did not raise any objection against the construction of atomic bombs.

But when Einstein heard about the dropping of the first atom bomb, he was deeply grieved. America's atomic scientists realized that they would have to share responsibility in this area. In May 1946 they organized the Emergency Committee of Atomic Scientists, with Einstein as its president. Acting in this capacity, he made a plea for world peace: "Our defense does not lie in arms, or science, or underground shelters; our defense lies in law and order."

Einstein now supported the ideal of world government. Despite his many warnings, he remained optimistic about the future: "The splitting of the atom need not destroy mankind nor endanger civilization any more than did the invention of the match. What happens next will depend on the quality of man's character, not on the quality of his technology."

From 1948 on, Einstein knew that his heart condition could spell death at any moment. But he continued to work tirelessly on his unified field theory until he died on April 18, 1955; the theory was never completed.

During that whole period he was well aware that he could be on the wrong track completely. These doubts came to the surface in many of his remarks. He once wrote: "We have only to consider the question of life to realize how terribly primitive our knowledge and science is. For life lies imbedded potentially in the atom, as the living being is in the fertilized ovum; the mystery of the whole is locked up in the elemental infrastructure. No matter how deeply we probe into the basic level, mathematics does not allow us to spell out the implications of the basic equations."

Einstein's general theory of relativity and his work on a general field theory have not gone unchallenged. Science has continued to make rapid strides, and many later physicists now regard Einstein as a traditionalist. But later experiments have provided strong corroboration for the special theory of relativity. The use of atomic energy in particular has confirmed Einstein's assumption that mass and energy are equivalent.

By contrast, Einstein's later preoccupations seem to be almost metaphysical in character. A Rabbi once sent this telegram to Einstein: "DO YOU BELIEVE IN GOD STOP ANSWER IN 50 WORDS." Einstein telegraphed this reply: "I BELIEVE IN SPINOZA'S GOD, A GOD WHO REVEALS HIMSELF IN THE HARMONY OF WHAT EXISTS BUT WHO DOES NOT GET INVOLVED WITH THE DEEDS AND DESTINY OF MEN." His attempt to provide a unified explanation of all physical phenomena was rooted in that belief. He could not accept the notion that God plays roulette with the world. He waited patiently for death, regarding it as a return into the ordered harmony of the universe.

On the surface, Einstein did not seem to have any close relationship with astronomy. Of course, astronomical observations did confirm the theory of relativity. They did verify the bending of light rays in the sun's gravitational field and the precession of Mercury's perihelion. But Einstein's relationship to astronomy actually ran much deeper, for he was seeking the uniform law that governed all things in the universe — from the smallest to the biggest. On a tour of Mount Wilson Observatory, Einstein and his wife were shown the huge reflecting telescope. His wife asked why the instrument was so big. The director explained that they were trying to establish the shape and makeup of the whole universe. Mrs. Einstein said quietly: "My husband works at that problem on the back of an old envelope."

Thanks to modern physics, astronomy has come a long way towards being astrophysics. It is an attempt to reach for the stars intellectually, to comprehend the star world with the aid of a single all-embracing law. Whether that can ever be achieved is a moot question. In *The Evolution Of Physics* (by Einstein and Infeld), Einstein compared the march of science to a detective story. Countless generations of scientists have tried to unlock the book of nature. Man has discovered more and more, yet the great mysteries remain unsolved. Einstein remarks: "We cannot say for sure that there is an ultimate solution."

MAN AND THE KNOWN UNIVERSE

As the size of the universe has shrunk for physics, it has grown greater for astronomy. Compared with the dimensions we discuss today, the reckonings of ancient and medieval times seem ridiculously small. No longer are earth and the heavens close neighbors. No longer can the gods leap to earth in a single bound. The realm of divine spirits, the roof of our earthly world, is no more.

Even Copernicus regarded the planetary system as the whole universe. The fixed stars did not concern him at all. Tycho Brahe and Kepler tried to measure movements in them. Giordano Bruno was the first to assert that the fixed stars could be other suns, circling in the cosmos at stupendous distances from one another. Around 1750 Thomas Wright ventured the notion that our solar system was only one part of a giant galaxy, our Milky Way, and that there were countless similar galaxies in the universe. This assumption, developed further by Immanuel Kant, has proved to be correct. Today we know that earth and the other planets are not the only rotating bodies. The sun, too, revolves around some distant center of the Milky Way at a velocity of 170 miles per second; one revolution takes about 200 million years.

A galaxy quite similar to our Milky Way is the Andromeda nebula. It is about 2.2 million light years away, and it has a diameter of approximately 110,000 light years. Using large telescopes, we can break down portions of it into individual stars and dark clouds.

Our stellar system and Andromeda, each with their 100,000 million suns, are not the whole universe. There are countless other systems, visible to our telescopes as hazy nebulae. In the nineteenth century they were numbered in thousands; today about 100 million of them have been detected. The dimensions of the stellar panorama have taken on awesome proportions.

The most distant galaxies so far detected are about 5 billion light years away. This means that the light we are receiving from them now started out 5 billion years ago, before the earth existed. It also means that even if we could travel at the velocity of light, it would take us 5 billion years to reach them.

So man, with the help of theories and instruments, has come to know the universe. He is even in a position to leave earth and travel in space. Yet, for all that, he seems more lost in space and time than ever before. Earth, once regarded as the center of the universe, has been reduced to an insignificant by-product of the cosmic process. The glaring sun has been demoted to the status of an average star.

In reaching for the stars, man's outlook has been radically transformed. His cosy world of heaven and earth has opened up into a vast, unlimited universe moving at headlong speed. His own existence has been downgraded in the process. Plunged amid all these endless galaxies, he knows that he is hardly the ruler of the universe. What is more, the fantasy about life on other stars has suddenly become a real possibility in this universe of countless galaxies.

Man will never be able to make direct contact with the deeper expanses of space. But the conquest of space by the human mind is something else. Geniuses like Isaac Newton and Albert Einstein give us a glimpse of the process. They could grasp the size and harmony of the vast stellar region, and relate it to their own moral outlook. While no mathematical law may ever be found to tie in the stars with Kant's ethical imperative, the search for such laws must count as one of man's nobler pursuits. The ultimate significance of space conquest is that it turns man's attention back to himself—to the conquest of his own spiritual and intellectual forces.

But the journey to the stars is under way. The first barriers have been overcome. Man has orbited earth and moon, and stepped out of his space vehicle into space itself. The dreams of the poets and the predictions of the scientists have been fulfilled. Around the same time that Einstein's mind was soaring above his contemporaries, the Wright brothers were rising from the ground at Kitty Hawk. While the new physics was taking shape in laboratories around the world, other men were developing the techniques of rockerty and electronic data-processing.

They all came together rather quickly. Scarcely fifty years after the first aeroplane flight, a man-made satellite rocketed beyond earth's gravitational field and orbited our planet. Man has always pushed beyond his limits. The more he gets to know them, the more determinedly he will seek to push them back.

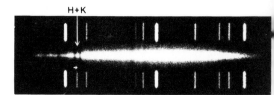

40 million light years   720 mi/sec.

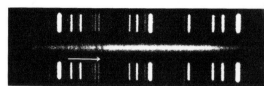

675 million light years   9,000 mi/sec.

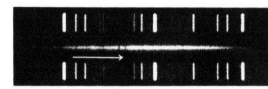

950 million light years   12,900 mi/sec.

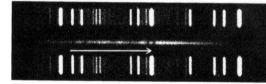

1700 million light years   23,400 mi/sec.

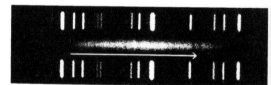

2700 million light years   36,600 mi/sec.

83. The spectra of the distant galaxies display a noteworthy phenomenon. The farther away they are, the more their spectral configuration moves towards the red end of the spectrum. Astrophysicists interpret this as a movement away from our galaxy. The pictures above depict a series of such spectra, indicating the distance of the galaxy and the shift to red (see arrow) caused by its velocity.

MODELS OF THE UNIVERSE

It was not until this century that scientists had enough physical and mathematical tools to probe the overall structure of the universe and provide some answers about it. Men had considered the question in earlier times, of course. Nicholas of Cusa pondered the spatial and temporal infinity of the universe. Giordano Bruno talked about the fixed stars as distant suns. He saw the universe as something infinite in size, unchanging in nature, and everlasting in duration; for this he was burned at the stake.

Such thoughts were shocking to the people of that era. They saw the fixed stars firmly attached to their special realm. Time and distance presented no pressing problem. Eventually, however, Bruno's ideas took hold on men's minds. Immanuel Kant was one of the first to look beyond the individual stars. Impressed with the star counts of F. W. Herschel, he asserted that the Milky Way was one of the basic building blocks of the universe, and that there were many millions of similar galaxies.

OLBERS' PARADOX

A German physician and amateur astronomer, Wilhelm Olbers (1758–1840), examined the consequences of Bruno's ideas. If the universe was infinite in space and time, then one had to face an insoluble contradiction. If these countless stars were distributed fairly evenly over the infinite universe, then from earth the heavens should be aglow with stars and there should be hardly any dark spots. The stars should be clustered together everywhere, yet this was not the case. Moreover, all the heavenly bodies ought to have reached a balance in temperature by now.

As everyone knows, however, the night sky is black; and a static, unchanging universe cannot last forever. Theory and observation did not agree. To solve this paradox, the German astronomer F. Zöllner (1834–1882) suggested that here we may be dealing with geometrical conditions that differ considerably from our traditional concepts of space. To support his theory, he introduced the notion of positively curved space. This notion was to be a result of the model of the universe inspired by the theory of relativity.

In non-Euclidean geometry Einstein found a suitable framework for his general theory of relativity. Space was non-Euclidean and positively curved. Such a conception of space cannot really be visualized in the ordinary way; it is accessible only in mathematical terms.

Admitting its deficiencies at the outset, we might venture to make the following comparison. A two-dimensional being (operating in the dimension of length and width) lives on a spherical surface and cannot leave it by going outward or inward. Moving on this surface (i.e. in two dimensional space), a being would never come to its end; the surface would appear to be unending. Moreover, he could always return to his starting point, no matter what direction he set out in. His straight lines are closed in upon themselves, and he would soon discover that the sum of the angles of a triangle is greater than 180°. This is the classical postulate for a spherical triangle. Thus our two-dimensional being lives: a) in a non-Euclidean world—the sum of the angles of a triangle in Euclidean space is exactly 180°; b) in a spherical world—the surface has a curve; c) in an unlimited world—it has no end point, but it is finite and can be measured; d) in a closed world—a straight line returns back on itself.

Now let us adapt this picture to three-dimensional beings like ourselves: a) Our space is non-Euclidean. The sum of the angles of a triangle is more than 180°. (This is so because parallel lines do not intercept in infinity in non-Euclidean geometry.) The relationship between the special theory of relativity and Newtonian mechanics is relevant here. In ordinary life on earth the angles of a triangle do add up to 180°. But when we start measuring triangles of millions of light years, the non-Euclidean character of the whole comes into play.

b) Our space is unlimited, but its overall magnitude is finite. Our earlier example of a spherical surface indicates what this means, and it is one of the most noteworthy and fascinating consequences to be derived from the notion of curved space. An unlimited but finite space frees us from all the difficulties of infinity, and it solves Olbers' paradox.

c) Our space is closed. If we could travel on a light ray (our straight line) at the speed of light, we would eventually return to our starting point. The trip, of course, would take billions of years.

The space we have sketched here has one characteristic that is particularly noteworthy. There is no essential change in its character when it expands, just as the surface of a balloon does not change essentially as you blow it up. And here we find a neat connexion with another phenomenon that has been observed in the spectral analysis of stars: the red shift.

When we overlap the spectra of individual stars, we get a spectrum of a stellar galaxy. These latter spectra show a red shift: the spectral lines tend towards long (red) wavelengths at one end of the spectrum. The farther away the galaxies are, the more marked the tendency is.

Now we know from physics that a light source moving *towards* the observer shows a spectral shift towards the short wave (violet) end of the spectrum; and we also know that a light source moving *away* from the observer shows a shift towards the long (red) wave-end of the spectrum. This phenomenon is called the Doppler effect—after the Austrian physicist, Christian Doppler (1803–1853).

Astrophysicists have every reason to assume that the red shift in the spectra of the galaxies is an instance of the Doppler effect. In other words, the red shift indicates that the distant galaxies are moving away from our own galaxy. Now this must be understood correctly. It is not true only in terms of the earth. Wherever one stood in the universe, one would get the impression that everything else was moving away from that point; and that the more distant galaxies were moving away faster (see picture page 164).

This red shift in the galaxies is now commonly interpreted as an expansion of space. It is sometimes called the *Hubble Effect*—after the American astronomer, Edwin Hubble (1889–1953). Since the universe, by definition, does not allow for anything outside itself, there is no sense in asking where the universe is going. But it is possible, of course, that the overall magnitude of the universe is increasing over the course of time.

AN EXPANDING UNIVERSE

Now what does it mean to talk about expansion in non-Euclidean, positively curved space of finite overall magnitude? Cosmology tries to provide some explanation, and it has evolved various models of the universe that differ in one or another respect. The distribution of matter in the universe and the presence or absence of intergalactic gas and dust are two items it must consider in this process.

Let us consider the simplest possible case, and some of the models proposed for it. At the outset, the universe was nothing more than a dot. It began to expand at some point in time into the phenomenon we see today. But this expansion does not go on for an infinite length of time; it gradually slows up and eventually will come to a standstill. Then a process of contraction will start and gather increasing momentum, until the universe has contracted to the dot from which it started. The life span of this pulsating universe is many, many billions of years.

Another model starts out with the same dot, but it pictures the expansion process continuing forever. One radical difference between the two models is this: in the second model, expansion does not involve any enlargement of space. An infinitely long expansion has an infinitely large space in which to take place; and

Graph of the red shift in km/sec (1 km = .62 miles) and its relation to distance in millions of light years. The red shift can be measured directly from the shift in spectral lines (see page 164).

infinite space cannot get any larger. Here expansion implies that the galaxies continue to move away from each other, so that the mean density of matter in the universe decreases steadily.

We may well wonder whether astronomy is in a position to say anything about one model or another. Numerical counts of the faintest (hence most distant) galaxies should yield some clues, but the usefulness of such data is minimal. The data from astronomical observation is too inexact and complicated, and it does not support one model to the exclusion of others. Up to now every observer finds confirmation for his model in the data he observes.

Some models of the universe — that of Hoyle, Bondi, and Gold, for example — have a Euclidean structure but free themselves from one of the basic postulates of physics. They assume that the law of the conservation of energy does not hold, and that new matter does appear in meager but regular amounts. Thus, despite the expansion of the universe, its mean density would remain just about the same. Exactly how this happens no one knows.

We can now summarize the three basic presuppositions which cosmology accepts in constructing models of the universe.
a) In the universe as a whole, matter and motion are evenly divided;
b) no particular property is superior to other properties;
c) the universe has no midpoint and no axis.
Clearly we have come a long way from the neat geocentric universe of bygone days.

The origin of the universe must remain an open question. Astronomy cannot say anything for sure about it. We are often tempted to equate the incipient expansion of the universe with its actual beginning, but we have no sure proof of that. From an analysis of the Hubble effect, we do know that between ten and twelve billion years ago the universe was jammed into a very narrow space and that it has been expanding ever since. Physics and astronomy can probe no farther back in time with the use of their methodologies. They can describe the present state of the universe, but they can only speculate about its beginning and its end.

TRAVEL IN SPACE

BY WERNHER VON BRAUN

Together with many other researchers over the past five centuries, the six men discussed here have provided us with a clear picture of the Earth's place in the universe. It is a tiny speck in space, but it is illumined by a consciousness of the awesomeness of creation.

Could man leave his home planet and venture out into the surrounding universe? Three men, who never knew each other personally, were the first to tackle this question scientifically. One was a Russian, one an American, and one a German.

THREE PIONEERS

84. Konstantin E. Tsiolkovsky. Besides his work in aerodynamics, his theory of reaction vehicles and his formula for cutoff velocity were basic to the development of rocketry.

Konstantin Eduardovich Tsiolkovsky was born near Ryazan, south of Moscow, in September 1857. His family was poor, but this did not dampen his early interest in physics and mathematics. His first work, dealing with the fundamentals of rocket propulsion, dates from August 25, 1898; but it was actually published five years later. Thus it took approximately two hundred years for someone to formulate a practical application of Newton's law of action versus reaction. Two other important contributions were offered by Tsiolkovsky: the notion of multi-stage rockets, and the idea of using liquid hydrogen and liquid oxygen as fuel. Tsiolkovsky died in Kaluga in 1935.

Robert Hutchings Goddard (1882–1945) came from Worcester, Massachusetts. He was twenty-five years younger than his Russian counterpart, and of a more practical bent. While Tsiolkovsky never tried to apply his theory, Goddard was a man who liked to experiment and to put his ideas to the test. His work in rocketry began around 1911. The first high point was the first successful launching of a liquid-fuel rocket on March 16, 1926. The rocket only got as high as 46 feet, but it was a start.

By 1937 Goddard was already using gyro-controlled rockets with automatic steering devices. In that year one of his rockets reached an altitude of almost two miles. A year later Goddard was working on pump-feeding mechanisms for rocket motors. During World War II, however, the American military showed little interest in long-distance rockets and their possible uses. They put Goddard to work developing catapult rockets designed to help launch airplanes. Goddard died right at the war's end—in August 1945.

Hermann Oberth, a Saxon, was born in 1894. His first achievement was the publication of a book on rockets and space travel—in 1923! In the book he tried to show scientifically that such rockets could be developed, and he even included a tentative sketch of one. It was a two-stage rocket, using alcohol and liquid oxygen in the first stage, liquid hydrogen and liquid oxygen in the second stage. In 1929 Oberth came to Berlin and was offered a chance to do experimental work along these lines. He gathered a group of young students and space enthusiasts around him, of which I was a member.

The head of the army testing department at that time was General Becker, an expert in ballistics and a professor at Berlin University. In 1932 he invited me to do doctoral work on the combustion process in rocket motors—to be financed by the war ministry. Becker had welcomed the concept of the liquid-fuel rocket as a substitute for long-range artillery, which had been forbidden by the treaty of Versailles. Thus, as Hitler built up the German war machine in the thirties, liquid-fuel rockets got particular attention. Our work at Kummersdorf and Peenemünde eventually led to the successful development of the liquid-fuel A-4 rocket, later known as the V-2. It could carry a 2000 pound warhead for a distance of 192 miles at supersonic speed.

In the postwar period, the victorious powers have put ever increasing importance on long-range rockets. Around 1950 the Soviet Union resolved to develop an arsenal of truly long-range rockets. (3,000 to 6,000 miles); the United States soon followed suit. It was this type of rocket that catapulted Sputnik I into space in 1957, and that has turned manned space flights into a reality. As the jet bomber paved the way for the jet passenger airliner, so the strategic rocket has paved the way for the peaceful conquest of space.

85. The first German mail rocket (1930); Professor Hermann Oberth is on the left. His name will always be linked with space flights because of his basic contributions. In 1923 he formulated the basic equation of rocketry. His principle of using multi-stage rockets suggested how huge payloads might be launched in the desired trajectory.

THE SPACEFLIGHT PROGRAM

Despite differences in detail, the basic aims of the spaceflight program are quite similar in the Soviet Union and the United States. We can distinguish three basic objectives in the peaceful exploration of space:

1. Unmanned spaceflights for scientific research. This is the goal behind many of the research satellites already in orbit. They are to provide astronomical, astrophysical, and geophysical data on numerous things: the structure of the earth's gravitational and magnetic field; cosmic radiation from the sun and the stars; the effect of solar wind and solar corpuscular radiation on the earth's magnetic field and its radiation belt.

This program includes moon probes, designed to chart its surface and to test potential landing surfaces. It also includes planetary probes, such as America's "Mariner" and Russia's "Zond" flights to Mars and Venus.

To what extent the Soviet Union is committed to further work along these lines, I do not know for sure. But indications are that it will be broadened to include even more distant planets. The United States have announced large-scale plans in this respect. There will be more "Voyager" trips around Mars between 1973 and 1979. Orbiting satellites will chart the surface of that planet, and biological laboratory

86. Robert Hutchings Goddard. His two main works on "a method of achieving higher altitudes" and "the development of liquid fuel rockets" describe his basic areas of concern. Interestingly enough, Goddard carried out his experiments in New Mexico, in an area close to White Sands, which is the present center of rocketry experimentation.

stations will eventually make soft landings there to study Martian forms of life. Other Voyager satellites will journey towards Venus and Mercury, and there are even plans for probing Jupiter, Saturn, Uranus, and Neptune.

2. Unmanned spaceflights for practical purposes. This category includes intelligence, television, weather, and navigational satellites. To these there will soon be added satellites for flight safety control, unmanned weather stations of a permanent nature, and satellites that will seek out untapped sources of raw materials on earth.

3. Manned spaceflights. Up to now these flights, both in the Soviet Union and the United States, have been designed to acquaint us with the general technical, medicinal, and operational problems of manned spaceflight. While it is true that we have not yet learned or mastered the whole problem of spaceflight, the Mercury and Gemini programs have taught us so much that we can now move on confidently to the more challenging goal of the Apollo program: the moon. It is almost certain that the Russian space program has put them in a similar position regarding an eventual landing on the moon.

Landing a man on the moon is often depicted as a race between the two great powers. This may well be true, insofar as it spurs both sides to put forth their best effort. But the real value of this endeavor is not tied up with the prestige of being first on the moon or with the scientific value of that first handful of moondust. The broader purpose of manned spaceflight was well put by President Kennedy: "We must learn to sail on the ocean of space."

We already have plans on paper to send not only instruments but also men to Mars. We are convinced that from a scientific and technological standpoint it should be possible to achieve this within the next twenty years—i.e. by 1987. Whether it actually is done or not will depend more on the willingness of the taxpayer than on the capability of the scientist.

87. Wernher von Braun. In 1942 he built the first successful V-2 liquid-fuel rocket at Peenemünde. Since the end of the war he has been deeply involved in American rocket development. In 1958 he sent the first American satellite, Explorer I, into orbit. Under his direction there developed the most powerful rocket boosters in the Western world.

FUTURE PROSPECTS

In the United States we have already begun to fuse the manned spaceflight program with spaceflights designed to promote scientific and economic purposes. Using the structural materials designed for the Apollo program, we have turned our attention in recent months to these items:

—An experimental space station, which could be manned by a crew for months as it orbited the earth.

—A solar observatory, attached to this space station, where trained astrophysicists could examine the sun in terms of X-rays, gamma rays, and distant ultraviolet. This can only be done outside the earth's atmosphere, which is impermeable for these rays.

—Also included in this station would be a series of special cameras and spectrally selective radiometers, focusing on the passing earth below. Using these devices, the crew could determine the best instruments to be used in future satellites designed to hunt for untapped raw materials.

MANNED SPACE FLIGHTS LEADING TO MOON LANDING

Launch Date	Spaceship	Crew	Orbits	Highest Altitude in miles
April 12, 1961	Vostok I (USSR)	Y. Gagarin	1	196.2
May 5, 1961	Liberty VII (USA)	A. Shephard	5-minute ballistics flight	108
July 21, 1961	Liberty Bell (USA)	V. Grissom	5-minute ballistics flight	108
Augurt 6, 1961	Vostok II (USSR)	G. Titov	17	145
February 20, 1962	Mercury VI (USA)	J. Glenn	3	166
May 24, 1962	Mercury VII (USA)	S. Carpenter	3	162
August 11, 1962	Vostok III (USSR)	A. Nikolayev	64 (rendezvous attempt)	136
August 12, 1962	Vostok IV (USSR)	P. Popovitch	48 (rendezvous attempt)	139
October 3, 1962	Mercury VIII (USA)	W. Schirra	6	178
May 15, 1963	Mercury IX (USA)	G. Cooper	22	166
June 14, 1963	Vostok V (USSR)	W. F. Bykovski	82 (rendezvous attempt)	131
June 16, 1963	Vostok VI (USSR)	V. W. Tereshkova (first woman in space)	48 (rendezvous attempt)	136
October 12, 1964	Voskhod I (USSR)	W. Komarov K. Feoktistov B. Yegorov	16	236
March 18, 1965	Voskhod II (USSR)	P. Belyayev A. Leonov (first man to walk in space)	17	297
March 23, 1965	Gemini III (USA)	V. Grissom J. Young	3	150
June 3, 1965	Gemini IV (USA)	A. McDivitt E. White (first American to walk in space)	66	175
August 21, 1965	Gemini V (USA)	G. Cooper C. Conrad (Simulated rendezvous)	120	190
December 4, 1965	Gemini VII (USA)	F. Borman J. Lovell	206	200
December 15, 1965	Gemini VI (USA)	W. Schirra T. Stafford (first complete rendezvous maneuver with Gemini VII)	16	169
March 16, 1966	Gemini VIII (USA)	N. Armstrong D. Scott (1st rendezvous and docking, forced landing)	7	186
June 3, 1966	Gemini IX (USA)	E. Cernan T. Stafford	45	170
July 18, 1966	Gemini X (USA)	J. Young M. Collins	43	472
September 12, 1966	Gemini XI (USA)	C. Conrad R. Gordon	44	855
November 11, 1966	Gemini XII (USA)	J. Lovell E. Aldrin	59	194
April 23, 1967	Soyuz 1 (USSR)	V. Komarov (killed on landing)	19	134
October 11, 1968	Apollo 7 (USA)	W. Schirra D. Eisele R. Cunningham	163 (rendezvous with booster rocket section)	282
October 25, 1968	Soyuz 3 (USSR)	G. Beregovoi	(rendezvous with unmanned Soyuz 2)	
December 21, 1968	Apollo 8 (USA)	F. Borman J. Lovell W. Anders	10 orbits around moon	70 from moon
March 3, 1969	Apollo 9 (USA)	J. McDivitt R. Schweickart D. Scott	151 (Practice separation of Lunar module, 113 miles apart)	300
May 18, 1969	Apollo 10 (USA)	T. Stafford J. Young E. Cernan	32 orbits round moon (Lunar module separation and rendezvous)	Command module 70 miles from moon Lunar module descends to 9 miles from moon
July 16, 1969	Apollo 11 (USA)	N. Armstrong M. Collins E. Aldrin	July 20 astronauts Armstrong and Aldrin land on the moon in their Lunar module. Neil A. Armstrong becomes first man to walk on the moon	

THE FIRST UNMANNED ROCKET LAUNCHINGS

March 16, 1926	First launching of liquid fuel rocket in Auburn, Massachusetts. Reaches altitude of approximately 46 feet.
May 31, 1935	Improved model of same rocket reaches altitude of over 7,600 feet.
February 24, 1949	Launching of first two-stage, liquid fuel rocket at White Sands, New Mexico. Reaches altitude of 240 miles.
August 22, 1951	A V-2 rocket reaches an altitude of 131.4 miles.
March 24, 1954	An American Viking 11 reaches altitude of 153 miles.
July 1956	A one-stage Aerobee-Hi attains the record altitude of 157.2 miles.
October 23, 1957	A four-stage, solid fuel rocket reaches altitude of 3,840 miles.

THE FIRST SIX SATELLITE LAUNCHINGS

October 4, 1957	First manmade satellite, Sputnik I (USSR), with a three-stage rocket.
November 3, 1957	Sputnik II (USSR).
February 1, 1958	Explorer I (USA).
March 17, 1958	Vanguard I (USA).
March 26, 1958	Explorer III (USA).
May 15, 1958	Sputnik III (USSR).

Right: On June 5, 1965, Edward White floated in space 96 miles above the earth. He was tethered to his Gemini capsule by a thin rope.

Next page: 180 miles above the earth, Gemini X, guided by John Young and Michael Collins, draws close for a rendezvous with its Agena target vehicle. When the two vehicles had docked, the Agena motor propelled them to a record altitude of 472 miles.

— A supply system, designed to provide the orbiting satellite with oxygen, food stuffs, and spare parts. This system would also relieve the crew at regular intervals, so that the service period would remain within reasonable limits.

There is a widespread but erroneous belief that space flight is much too expensive in terms of any practical benefits it may bring. To be sure, the initial development of space technology will cost billions of dollars. But development and practical exploitation are two different things. The cost of fuel for launching a satellite into orbit is enormous; but once the spacecraft is in orbit, it can stay there forever without consuming any additional fuel. Clearly, then, the use of some long-standing or permanent spacecraft system (e.g. a weather satellite system) will be incomparably cheaper in the long run than the use of regular aeroplane flights for the same purpose.

And so we head out to visit other planets in space, and to examine our own planet from a broader, cosmic perspective. Before us lie new possibilities that can bring rich benefits to mankind. Future historians will surely decide that the start of space travel was a turning point in the destiny of mankind.

MAN ON THE MOON

*"That's one small step for a man,
one giant leap for mankind."*

"That's one small step for a man, one giant leap for mankind", was Apollo 11 Commander Neil A. Armstrong's comment, as with one foot on one of Eagle's four 37″-diameter landing pads he probed the moon's surface layer of dust with the other. The time was 10.56 EDT on Sunday, July 20, 1969 (3.56 a.m. [B.S.T.], Monday, July 21). Eight years earlier, President Kennedy had given Nasa the official go-ahead for an amazing space programme that with almost incredible efficiency was to realize an ambition man had dreamed of for centuries. It is remarkable enough that Nasa should have achieved its immediate target within such a short time and with such precision (the moon landing, for instance, took place 30 seconds behind schedule), but perhaps even more astounding that this has been done with only one major tragedy—the deaths in January 1967 of Virgil Grissom, Roger Chaffee and Edward White in a launch-pad flash fire.

When Neil A. Armstrong, Edwin Aldrin and Michael Collins took off in Apollo 11 from the Cape Kennedy launch site on 16 July, they had ahead of them four major tasks that previous Apollo missions had prepared for, but not themselves attempted to achieve. They had to land on the moon, explore its surface, blast off again and conclude the latter manoeuvre by successfully docking with the mother ship, Columbia. The entire eight-day journey was watched by hundreds of millions of people throughout the world on television, and even when Apollo 11 was out of view of the launch-site spectators, a spotter plane's cameras took over and showed television viewers the first stage separation.

At launch, the clockwork precision that has characterized these Apollo missions operated again as the 3,100-ton craft gathered speed under the 7.5 million pound thrust of the Saturn 5 rocket's five engines.

The craft reduced speed from 5,000 to 3,600 mph as it began its first lunar revolution on an elliptical course 68 and 170 miles from the moon. On the third revolution the engine was fired again to put the craft into a near circular orbit some 70 miles above the surface.

Parallel to these events another drama was taking place. The Russians had surprised the world shortly before the Apollo lift-off by announcing the launch of Luna 15, an unmanned craft. Some people feared that it might attempt to steal the Americans' thunder by soft-landing on the moon and returning to earth with rock samples before Apollo 11 had completed its mission. Though the Russians were at first silent about Luna 15's objectives, the Americans were assured that there would be no interference. (A few hours after Eagle's lift-off from the moon the Russians announced that Luna 15 landed on the moon and had thus completed its mission.)

On 20 July, four days out from Cape Kennedy, having previously checked that all was well with the Lunar landing module, first Edwin Aldrin and then, an hour later, Neil Armstrong, clambered through the hatch from Columbia into Eagle, where they spent several hours checking everything again, and preparing for separation. Michael Collins stayed behind in Columbia to await their return. On the thirteenth orbit Columbia and Eagle separated successfully, and later Armstrong fired the control rockets that put Eagle into the correct pre-descent position.

Later, Armstrong fired the descent engine so as to slacken Eagle's speed and take it out of lunar orbit down towards the surface, at what seemed like horrifying speeds, until around 1,500 feet the craft slowed down appreciably. Twelve minutes after the firing of the descent engine Eagle landed safely in the Sea of Tranquillity. Armstrong later reported that there were several alarm signals during the final descent stage. He also had to take over from the onboard computer so as to avoid the possibly disastrous landing site towards which the computer flight path was taking them.

The first words from man on the moon were: "Houston. Tranquillity base. The Eagle has landed." The astronauts did without the scheduled rest period and instead made preparations for their moon walk. Armstrong was the first to climb down the ladder to the moon's surface, and he was soon followed by Aldrin. Each carried a 120-pound backpack that contained their oxygen supply, communications equipment, coolant system and several controls and instruments. The astronauts reported that they experienced no difficulty in coping with the one-sixth gravity of the moon, and earth viewers could see this for themselves when the astronauts deployed television cameras on the moon's surface. They carried out as many of the scheduled experiments as they had time for. These included the gathering of lunar rock samples, the setting up of an earth-moon range-finding mirror operated through laser beams directed from earth, and a lunar earthquake detector, which was soon yielding information of great interest to scientists. When these exercises and experiments were completed, the astronauts climbed carefully back into Eagle. After further checks inside the craft, the ascent engine was fired and the upper section of the craft was blasted from the lower section at a speed that quickly reached 4,000 mph. They had been on the moon's surface 21 hours.

On Thursday, July 24, the lunar explorers landed safely in the Pacific some thirteen miles from the recovery vessel U.S.S. Hornet.

The Apollo 11 mission was rated an almost total success, and Nasa immediately released information about future plans. Space technologists are quickly becoming familiar with the problems involved and are now able to consider the exploration of Mars and the establishment of relay-manned space observatories with a confidence that would have been called folly a few years ago.

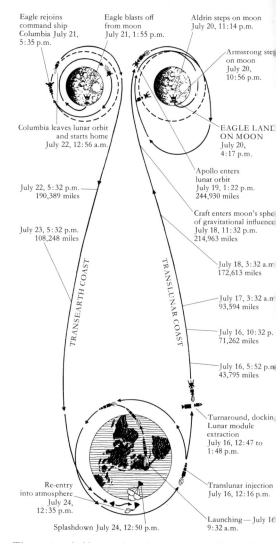

Eagle rejoins command ship Columbia July 21, 5:35 p.m.

Eagle blasts off from moon July 21, 1:55 p.m.

Aldrin steps on moon July 20, 11:14 p.m.

Armstrong steps on moon July 20, 10:56 p.m.

Columbia leaves lunar orbit July 22, 12:56 a.m.

EAGLE LANDS ON MOON July 20, 4:17 p.m.

July 22, 5:32 p.m. 190,389 miles

Apollo enters lunar orbit July 19, 1:22 p.m. 244,930 miles

July 23, 5:32 p.m. 108,248 miles

Craft enters moon's sphere of gravitational influence July 18, 11:32 p.m. 214,963 miles

TRANSEARTH COAST

TRANSLUNAR COAST

July 18, 3:32 a.m. 172,613 miles

July 17, 3:32 a.m. 93,594 miles

July 16, 10:32 p.m. 71,262 miles

July 16, 5:52 p.m. 43,795 miles

Turnaround, docking, Lunar module extraction July 16, 12:47 p.m. to 1:48 p.m.

Re-entry into atmosphere July 24, 12:35 p.m.

Translunar injection July 16, 12:16 p.m.

Launching—July 16 9:32 a.m.

Splashdown July 24, 12:50 p.m.

The previous double page shows left: Astronaut Edwin Eugene Aldrin standing beside a leg of the Lunar landing module during his moon walk. The astronauts' footsteps in the moon dust can be clearly seen. Right: Astronaut Edwin Eugene Aldrin beside the American flag (photos taken by Neil A. Armstrong, dpa/Nasa).

Page "Man on the Moon": The Lunar module of the Apollo mission 50,000 feet above the moon (photo: Nasa).

The crew of Apollo 11. Left to right: Neil A. Armstrong, Michael Collins and Edwin Eugene Aldrin (photo: Nasa).

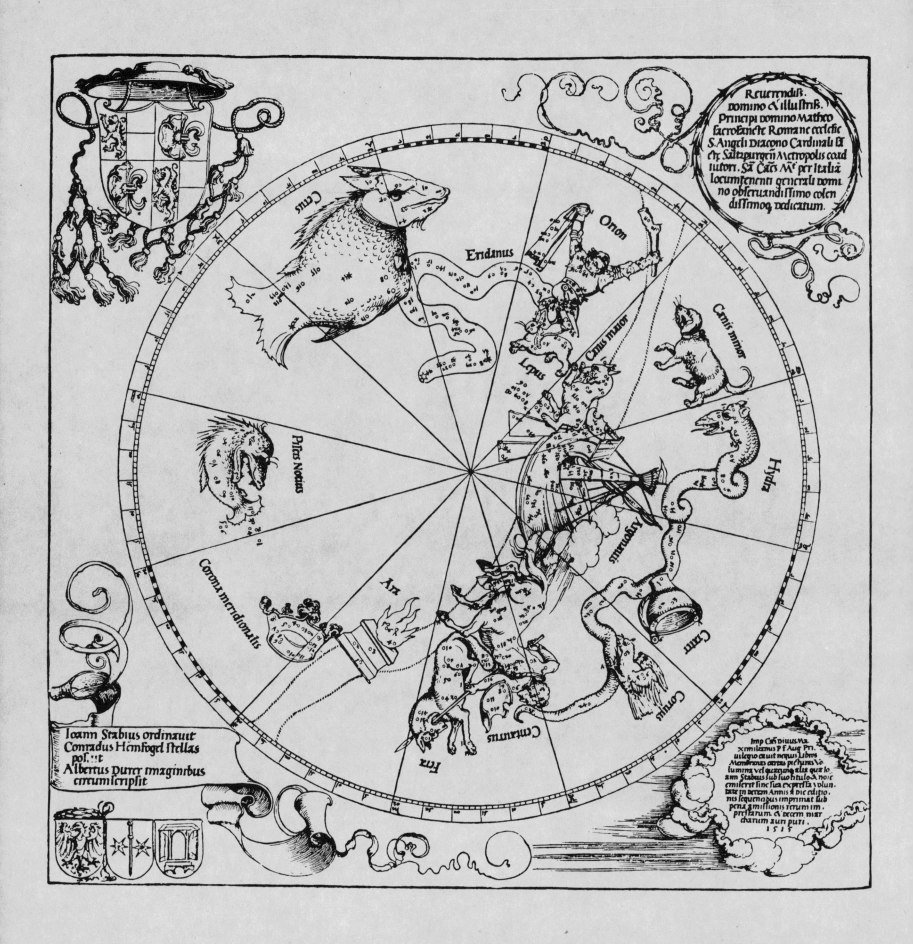